MANGO moment

MANGO moment

A small act of kindness & leadership

KRIS VANHAECHT

in collaboration with Elly Van Bael, Deborah Seys, Ellen Coeckelberghs, Charlotte van der Auwera, Eva Marie Castro and Filip Decruynaere

Acco Leuven / Den Haag

First edition: 2020

Published by

Uitgeverij Acco, Blijde Inkomststraat 22, 3000 Leuven, Belgium

Email: uitgeverij@acco.be – Website: www.acco.be

FSC www.fsc.org MIX Papier van verantwoorde herkomst FSC® C105389

The Netherlands:

Acco Nederland, Westvlietweg 67 F, 2495 AA Den Haag, The Netherlands

Email: info@uitgeverijacco.nl – Website: www.accouitgeverij.nl

Cover design: Frisco-ontwerpbureau

Typesetting: Press Point.be

Cover image: © Kris Vanhaecht

D/2020/0543/170 NUR 860 ISBN 978-94-6344-021-9

CONTENTS

REFLECTION *moment* OF...

FOREWORD

MANGO moment

Almost every corporate vision or mission statement will tell you that the customer is king. It's actually a bit of a cliché and it would be rather odd if the focus of a healthcare organisation were not on its patients. After all, they are surrounded by a whole army of experts and given the best possible care. But maybe the question we should be asking is whether the same attention is given to the human being behind the patient. That's what this book on Mangomoments, is all about.

In this era of technological progress, artificial intelligence, genetics and electronics, the patient is often reduced to a collection of blood counts, radiological images and clinical descriptions. Doctors, nurses and other caregivers do their utmost to explain this in human language and try to get everyone involved in the treatment or the process. But, when you find yourself in a vulnerable situation, is this really enough?

Healthcare facilities disconnect the patient from their environment, their trusted partner, and their friends. Sometimes it's only when the cleaner makes their daily visit that the patient has any contact with someone from the hospital who is not intent on providing treatment. This contact with everyday normality can be calming and reassuring. A glimpse of humanity, a joke, a small gesture: offering just that little bit more than routine care and taking a friendly approach instead of merely providing clinical empathy often make all the difference. These small, attentive gestures sometimes work miracles and can have a major impact on the motivation of the patient or resident, often putting the sparkle back in their eyes.

The term 'Mangomoments' refers to gestures like this, when someone pays some attention to the human being behind the patient, thereby shifting the focus to the human side of healthcare.

This book brings together a collection of stories, scientific insights and critical reflections. After the introduction by two international experts, Professor Kris Vanhaecht explains how it all started, followed in the next section by thirteen inspiring stories about warm-hearted care sent to us by patients, family members and healthcare professionals. The team that carried out the research about Mangomoments, which was only possible thanks to the support of Kom op tegen Kanker (Stand Up to Cancer), developed the Mangomoment model. This book also covers the various aspects of this model and how it came into being. Finally, we asked twenty-nine experts from all over the world to reflect on Mangomoments, based on their role and perspective. These reflections, from the point of view of patient, company, management and healthcare professional offer you a number of building blocks that may help you to find a place for Mangomoments within your own organisation. The final series of reflections highlight the fact that Mangomoments have a wider applicability than the care sector alone. The final word is left to Stand up to Cancer, the organisation that made it possible for the Mangomoment to grow from an idea into the movement it is today.

The aim of the KU Leuven Institute for Healthcare Policy (LIHP) in publishing this book and establishing the KU Leuven Mangomoment Fund is to support and disseminate a positive healthcare message. More information about the Fund can be found at www.mangomoment.org.

The beneficial effects on patient motivation, but also on the motivation of staff and the healthcare institution itself are worthy of further study. The academics in question will continue to work hard on this.

The most important message of this book, however, is that behind every patient is a flesh-and-blood human being who needs those small, friendly and familiar gestures to keep them optimistic about the future.

So, don't lose sight of the human being behind the patient!

Prof. Dr. Dirk De Ridder
Head of Department at the
KU Leuven Institute for Healthcare Policy

PREFACE

Pedro Delgado, head of Europe and Latin America, Institute for Healthcare Improvement, Boston.

Maureen Bisognano, president emerita, Institute for Healthcare Improvement, Boston & Faculty member of the Harvard TH Chan School of Public Health, Boston.

When Kris first told me about Mangomoments, memories flooded in for me. I, Pedro Delgado, grew up in Venezuela, where mangos can be grabbed off trees everywhere. I ate them at every stage of their development – from green (harder, more acidic) to yellow (softer, sweet) – with the same amount of pleasure and, more importantly, with freedom and joy. As I developed my throwing and catching skills, higher-up mangos became targets for long-distance throws. My friends and I used to compete for who could get more mangos "down", and once we knocked them loose, who could catch more mangos as they fell. The objective was to protect them from hitting the ground as they fell, since the impact could damage their lovely shape and texture. A few years ago, during a senior leadership meeting with healthcare executives in Singapore, I heard a slight bang on the roof and asked what happened. Our hosts explained that branches of a mango tree reached above the small building, and mangos often fell. I couldn't stop myself from describing my mango memories. To my surprise, 15 minutes later they brought in a tray of the fallen mangos, sliced up for the afternoon break. Pure joy. The memories generated an emotional response to Kris' moving story –

I found Mangomoments instantly appealing and incredibly moving. When Kris told Maureen about this idea, she too experienced a similar connection to heart and mind.

In our work on healthcare improvement across the globe, we have promoted patient-centredness as a cornerstone of improvement and leadership, one of the six Institute of Medicine domains of healthcare quality, clearly interconnected with dignity and Joy in Work. We support the annual 'What Matters to You?' day, now a global movement. We've witnessed the evolution from patient engagement to partnership with patients, along with the increased practice of co-design and co-production of health and care. These are concepts and practices closely connect with the values of love, equity, trust and courage of the Institute of Healthcare Improvement (IHI). Furthermore, they're concepts that have a mutually beneficial and reinforcing positive effect for patients and healthcare professionals. We've learned that in leadership it takes courage to let go, to share or cede control to those we serve, and to include patient-centredness and partnership into daily practice in healthcare. And the evidence for leaders is clear: compassion in care is improving patient experiences, decreasing medical errors, and is a powerful tool to decreasing costs in healthcare - a sure path to achieving IHI's Triple Aim.

Mangomoment stories from this book are moving, a source of hope and inspiration for us all. As Dr. Barbara Fredrickson argues, for human beings to flourish, we need to get essential daily nutrients — not only from food, but also from a laugh, a hug or even a smaller moment of positive emotion, especially with someone with whom we click. Healthcare professionals are ideally placed to touch people's lives at times of vulnerability by going above and beyond treating core physical symptoms and suffering. As you'll read throughout this book, simple questions can evoke fascinating exchanges, and open surprising opportunities to activate pathways of mutual compassion, gratefulness and appreciation. We love the simplicity of the Mangomoment concept, and its international adoption is testament to how pragmatic it is, and how much appetite exists for creating extraordinary moments as part of what we do daily in healthcare. The book also contains deep reflections from leaders that invite us all to consider additional angles to Mangomoments and underline their relevance in today's efforts towards better care, better health and sustainable costs.

The cost and availability of mangos globally varies greatly. The good news for healthcare is that Mangomoments do not need a tropical climate to thrive – they need a receptive environment and a desire for making every single patient experience extraordinary. We all stand to gain hugely from the benefits of these special, sacred moments. We dream of a future where Mangomoments are not an exception but a self-embraced rule, with millions of professionals and patients reaping the benefits of compassion and positive resonance daily. Let's accept the gift of Mangomoments and the invitation to make them available everywhere and start to write a new chapter for healthcare of partnership, full of stories that in the future, will allow our memories to be flooded with interactions that enriched lives at the time and forever.

HOW IT ALL BEGAN...

MANGO moment

Two months after awaking from a coma in the intensive care unit, Viviane described how hard she had found it lying in bed with nothing to do but listen to the alarms from all the equipment and stare at the white ceiling. She spoke of seeing deceased family members standing by her bed and hearing their voices. And of how she considered asking for euthanasia. But during the same interview Viviane also talked about gradually starting to enjoy life's little pleasures again, such as eating a meal or just looking out the window.

In 2015, Viviane shared these experiences with Annemie Struyf, a journalist of the Flemish public broadcast service VRT. Her testimony was part of a gripping documentary entitled 'Via Annemie' about life in intensive care at the University Hospitals Leuven. Clearly touched by Viviane's story, Annemie paused during the interview before asking: "Is there anything you're looking forward to?" Viviane thought for a moment and then responded: "A mango, I would love to taste a mango again." At the end of filming, Annemie paid Viviane another visit, this time bringing a mango as a gift. It was Viviane's turn to be touched. Moved to tears by this small gesture she said: "I'll never, ever forget this!"

When I watched the documentary, I was confused. Why hadn't any of Viviane's caregivers known that a mango was all it would take to make Viviane so happy? And how could a small gift give a patient such a positive experience? Or was it just because it was Annemie Struyf, a well-known journalist? I contacted Annemie and told her about my work as a professor at the KU Leuven Institute for Healthcare Policy on topics such as quality of care, patient safety incidents and second victims. I asked her if this 'Mangomoment' had been staged or had come about spontaneously. "Of course it was spontaneous. It just happened. There was a positive chemistry between us", was Annemie's answer.

The documentary gave me the idea of introducing the Mangomoment concept. At first, responses tended to be negative. I was told it was a silly and unscientific idea and faced comments such as 'Why focus so much on this? We're all doing our best, aren't we? And we're already so busy.' But after conversations with my colleague Barbara, who suggested the name Mangomoment, my dear daughter Manon, who at the age of 10 clearly understood what Mangomoment was all about, and some passionate doctors and patients, I felt we needed to do something more with it. I got my academic team all fired up about the idea and we put our heads together and refused to give up. We persisted and initiated a project at three Flemish hospitals, the University Hospitals Leuven, the General Hospital Diest and the Imelda Hospital Bonheiden. This project that was made possible by the financial support of Stand up to Cancer. The pilot in three hospitals grew into a person-centred movement involving more than fifty healthcare organisations from Flanders and the Netherlands. In January 2018, we published an article in *The Lancet Oncology*, a top scientific medical journal. This brought the Mangomoment international attention and we suddenly found ourselves being taken seriously by the academic world. More than a year later we completed the study 'From Never to Always Events: in search of Mangomoments'. Thanks to our campaign within healthcare organisations and via social media, we have collected 1,045 Mangomoment stories that were donated by patients and their relatives and caregivers. The research team conducted 120 in-depth interviews and organised four focus groups. In December 2018, 'Mangomoment' was just pipped at the post as the word of the year in Flanders, and took third place in the Netherlands. With the concept receiving increasing interest from abroad, we still don't know where this story will end. Mangomoment was mentioned during conferences and symposia all over the world by global leaders in healthcare management. The original video with Annemie and Viviane, which is available at www.mangomoment.org, has been used worldwide by our Mangomoment ambassadors. A Dutch book on Mangomoments was launched in June 2019, and my daughter Manon handed over the first book to Viviane. This gesture too, both will never forget. More than 1,000 people followed the live streaming on Facebook of the presentation of the book and the inauguration of the Mangomoment Fund. This KU Leuven Fund will support research and teaching on person-centred care. In October 2019 we received an additional grant from Stand Up To Cancer to launch Mangomoment Inspiration Workshops in forty healthcare organisations and collaborate with them for the next three years. In this new project we will search for a Mangomoment Culture and we will develop the Mangomoment Culture Scale. We spoke at many conferences and we had the privilege to see and feel how people, young and old, clinicians and managers, patients and family, the ill and healthy, were all touched by the Mangomoment movement. Nowadays we receive more and more questions and feedback from companies outside healthcare as Mangomoments touch their general management and leadership challenges.

The publication of this English book is an important step towards anchoring those little courtesies and gestures into the quality policy of any warm-hearted organisation worldwide.

The Mangomoment book

In writing this new book, we hope to provide inspiration, motivation and food for thought for current and future patients, nursing home residents, home care providers, general hospitals, and providers of psychiatric and rehabilitation care, as well as those caring for the disabled. Inspiration from the many beautiful stories about Mangomoments that were sent to us. Motivation to give person-centredness a central role in the field of healthcare quality. And food for thought for readers reflecting how they can and want to work together towards more warm-hearted care based on their own unique role in the healthcare sector. Moreover, these stories and reflections are also meant to inspire the workforce and leadership team from service industry outside healthcare.

I would like to offer my sincere thanks to everyone who has shared stories, and especially the people whose stories we selected for publication in the book. These are just a few of the more than a thousand stories that inspired us; they could have come from any organisation worldwide and will as such be familiar to many caregivers, patients and family members. We are, of course, grateful to Annemie Struyf for inspiring us, and to the one and only Viviane for her enthusiasm, her ambassadorship of the Mangomoment concept, and her warm friendship. I would also like to thank all employees and contacts in the partner organisations and the members of our advisory board. A special thank you to my international friends and mentors. Without them, 'Mangomoments' would never have become the movement it is today.

We are grateful to the authors of the reflections for presenting their visions and helping you, the reader, to reflect on the future of customer centricity. I would like to thank all the staff at KU Leuven who, each based on their own expertise, made this book, the Mangomoment movement and the Mangomoment Fund possible. We are also grateful to our financial ambassadors Emeritus Professor Collen, law firm Dewallens en Partners, as well as Best Choice by Special Fruit.

All proceeds from this book will be donated to the KU Leuven Mangomoment Fund.

Finally, I would like to thank the whole team of Stand Up To Cancer for giving this crazy idea such a unique opportunity and for continuing to believe in the campaign, the search for stories and the implementation of Mangomoments.

Just a coincidence...?

I'm still wondering whether it was a coincidence that Viviane was longing for a mango. In October 2017, during our campaign, the film Victoria & Abdul, starring Dame Judi Dench and focussing on the relationship between the queen and her servant, was showing in cinemas. Walking through the park, Victoria asks: "A mango, what is it?" Abdul answers: "The queen of fruit! In India, gifting a basket of mangos is considered a gesture of friendship. The sacred mango tree is a symbol of love." The trailer closes with the words: "A queen for a queen. Abdul introduced Victoria to the mango, and made the world a little sweeter."

Maybe it's time to put healthcare in a more positive light too. After all the – sometimes negative – reports in the media about medical errors, staffing shortages, burnout and financial difficulties, these positive Mangomoments allow us to learn from each other and inspire one another even in healthcare organisations. Or as we concluded in The Lancet: "Mangomoments can help us to make healthcare a little sweeter." And maybe this is not only our wish for healthcare but also for all organisations were kindness and leadership may enhance the quality of life for all stakeholders.

I wish you happy reading and hope you find inspiration and food for thought in the search for more warm-hearted care.

Prof. Dr. Kris Vanhaecht,
associate professor in quality and patient safety,
KU Leuven

"Mangomoments are small, unexpected, surprising, sometimes almost imperceptible actions, courtesies or gestures between patients, residents, family members and/or care providers during the day-to-day provision of care. They don't take a lot of time, resources or energy and create a positive bond between those involved."

More information: www.mangomoment.org

THE MANGO *moment* OF...

© Photo News

THE MANGOMOMENT OF

ILSE AND EMMA

MANGO *moment*

IT'S WONDERFUL JUST TO FEEL LIKE AN ORDINARY MUM AGAIN

MANGO moment

"We were about to go on holiday with the family. I was very tired and went to see my doctor for a blood test. The result was worrying. Further tests quickly followed, as did the diagnosis: acute myeloid leukaemia at an advanced stage. My husband and I just sat there, totally stunned. The diagnosis called for urgent treatment, but the doctor let us go home first so we could explain things to our children ourselves. When we got the news, our daughter was celebrating her birthday party. So my husband and I went out for a lovely meal, just the two of us. We drank champagne and ate lobster. After the party, we told the children what was going on. I was very happy that the doctor gave us the opportunity to do that, rather than admitting me straight into hospital, even though that would have been better from a strictly medical point of view.

During my stay on the isolation ward, my children were allowed to visit from time to time. Young children are normally banned from the ward to eliminate risk, but the doctor would turn a blind eye every now and then to lift my spirits. If you have to stay in isolation for two months, every bit of contact is important, even when it comes via Facebook. If you're feeling lonely or ill during the night, one of your contacts is bound to be awake somewhere, and you feel less alone when someone responds. The night nurses are also a source of support. There was one in particular that I had a very good relationship with, and I often lay awake at night waiting for her to come round. Even today, I still keep in touch with at least ten caregivers on Facebook."

Your life in their hands

"It should come as no surprise that you develop a strong bond with the healthcare team: you have to rely so much on them. Your life really is in their hands to a certain extent. A nurse once made a mistake when setting up my chemotherapy. The whole of the chemotherapy agent was released into my body over a single hour instead of the four hours it was supposed to take. She was devastated and almost couldn't face me. But I couldn't be mad at her – she was a kind-hearted and dedicated woman. And, yes, it was scary. But it didn't kill me, so we just moved on with things. The bond you have with the team makes a big difference.

I have always tried to be friendly to doctors, nurses and cleaning staff, even when things weren't going well. If you are kind to people, they tend to be kind to you. You can't imagine how important it is for doctors and caregivers to treat you as a human being as well as a patient. You want the doctor to explain your white blood cell count and tell you about the extra bags of blood you need, but you also want them to ask: 'And how are you today? How are you feeling?' That concern, that consideration is highly appreciated. It keeps you feeling like a human being. It makes all the difference."

Coke and crisps with the curtains shut

"It's the little things that count. That time when my 11-year-old daughter Emma was allowed to stay a little longer, and we watched a film together on my laptop. Me on the bed, her sitting next to me with crisps and a can of coke, and we drew the curtains just for fun. The film was *Pride and Prejudice* – we'd both seen it before, but that didn't matter. It was just a lovely mother-daughter moment. The care team made sure we weren't disturbed. Heavenly! For a moment, I just felt like an ordinary mum again.

Or the time a nurse gave me a little massage. I still get goose bumps thinking about that. She had actually just come to make my bed, but she saw that I wasn't feeling great. So she spontaneously offered to give me a little massage. Talk about a Mangomoment! To eliminate risk, as few people as possible are admitted. Once someone from a volunteer association was allowed to give me a manicure. Nail painting, the whole works. It's usually not my kind of thing, but at that time it helped me a lot. Just to feel like a woman again. And to have someone touch me, just for a moment, without any risk. That manicure took only half an hour, but the effect lasted much longer. At the time it was an incredible experience.

I am also grateful to the cleaning staff for the beautiful moments they gave me. They have nothing to do with all the medical stuff, but ultimately, they are the ones who are in your room for the longest. And they chat about the ordinary things in life while they're getting their jobs done. It seems so normal, but it's those moments when you feel like you're a human being and not just a patient. It's those moments that give you strength."

© Rob Stevens

ANNEMIE MANGO moment

MANGO moment

TRUST IS A TWO-WAY STREET

"In 1993 I had an accident while on a gymnastics internship in the Czech Republic. I was seventeen at the time. I did a double forward somersault that went wrong and I've been paralysed from the neck down ever since. I can't breathe on my own and I'm in a wheelchair. But I didn't just lay down. I became a business engineer in computer sciences and gained a master's degree in healthcare management and policy. Then I got my PhD in biomedical sciences. Nowadays I work as a researcher at KU Leuven.

During my time in intensive care, I experienced a fantastic Mangomoment. In the old ward I was on after my accident, there was a lot of light in the rooms. Too much, in fact – it gave me a headache and the curtain barely shut out the sun. To remedy that, the nurses hung up an extra sheet, which helped. After a while, someone drew something on the sheet. Then someone saw it and added some text. After a few days the sheet was full of drawings and writing. I loved that; it was such a personalised curtain! Even after all these years, I've still got that sheet. I can't bring myself to throw it away. It meant so much to me."

Feeling welcome

"I was very ill at the time, with one infection after another. I was on various different kinds of antibiotics and my kidneys failed. I had to stay in hospital for a long time. I knew the people there very well and they knew me. Every time I went back, they hung up a banner to welcome me. It was heart-warming. It makes an incredible difference when you walk in somewhere and immediately feel welcome. When people show that they're expecting you and are happy to see you. It makes your stay in hospital less stressful, less charged. I had some lovely moments with a lot of those nurses.

The bond between nurse and patient can be very special, especially at night. That's when the visitors stop coming and you are completely dependent on that one person. My experiences of that have been quite mixed. There were some wonderful nurses, who I got along with very well. But there were also some who were less friendly, and some I was even a bit afraid of. It's normal for some people to get along better than others, but you quickly get a sense of whether a doctor or nurse's heart is really in their job or not.

This is particularly true when it's busy on the ward. That's when there's less time for the nice little touches and that extra bit of attention. When it's busy, I don't ring the bell much. Only for aspiration, because I really need that. But you soon find out who you can turn to. There are some caregivers who always have time for you and there are some who are constantly stressed out and pressured; who chase around after each other a lot and shout at each other for no real reason. I see that on the haemodialysis ward, too. I don't think the staff themselves are aware of it, because it's all around them. But viewed from the outside, it's very obvious. As a patient, you soon get to know who you can count on and who you can't."

Trust works both ways

"At the time of the Mangomoment I already had a very good relationship with the team and we had gone through a lot together. Good moments, but also very bad periods and real lows. You share those experiences and the feeling never goes away. It's hard to put into words, but you can feel it. At around the same time, someone with a guitar put on a surprise concert in my room and a few of the nurses came to listen. That was another Mangomoment to store away and never forget.

When pancakes were being cooked on the ward, the nurses spontaneously came by. Those are the things that stay with you. They make you feel integrated, part of the team, even if you're a patient. Sometimes, I wonder if this boundary between caregivers and patient is really necessary – after all, you are working together. Some people are really good at getting you involved in an easy and natural way. I appreciate that. As a patient, you have to reveal a lot about yourself, and caregivers don't have to reciprocate. I understand that. Privacy is important. But still: trust works both ways, it's a matter of give and take. It should be possible to have an ordinary conversation with each other. As a patient, and as a human being, I need that sense of trust. And it works both ways: I think much more of nurses who open up to me than I do of their colleagues who don't show me that trust.

Being there for the patient

"Taking time for a patient ... it should be the most normal thing in the world. Some caregivers sense that perfectly and are really there for you. But that's not true of everyone. Some professionals seem to work on autopilot most of the time even though they are first and foremost human beings. We now have a 'What matters to you?' day once a year when they cook chips and give the patients some pampering. But, to me, this misses the point a bit, because you might still get a nurse at your bedside later on who is unfriendly or just not very interested. Being there for the patient is an ongoing process. Being friendly and respectful costs nothing. But it's so important and means such a lot.

It's really the little things that make the difference. The nurse who spontaneously goes to the vending machine to get me a drink. The nurse who had some free time and came to my room to read when I was very ill. It was reassuring just having someone around. A small gesture, but twenty years later I still know who that was. You never forget the real Mangomoments."

© Rob Stevens

THIBAUT MANGO *moment*

THE WONDERFUL STORIES COME FOR FREE

MANGO moment

"As a general practitioner, you often don't have to look very hard for an opportunity to give someone a Mangomoment. I had an 89-year-old patient who suffered from a fall and was in hospital with a broken shoulder. I wanted to call in, and bought an orchid in the hospital shop as a little gift. I thought it was a bit of a boring present, but to her it was a lovely, thoughtful thing to do, and she still has the orchid in her room at the residential care centre. She appreciated that little gesture enormously. I actually hadn't given much thought to what effect the gift might have, I just thought it might be nice to have a flower in your room when you have nothing to do but lie in bed. But, to that lady, the orchid meant so much more. Of course, as a general practitioner, you don't have to do that for every patient. But sometimes a token of attention can do a lot of good. Especially with older people, I suppose. I'll take the time to sit down. That's part of it, too."

I wouldn't say no to an eclair with my coffee

"On one occasion, I saw an elderly couple visiting the residential care centre. I was just passing and noticed that the man and woman were carrying a whole box of delicious cakes. They explained that every time they go, they bring tasty eclairs to enjoy with the residents. It creates a fantastic feel-good moment that they never get tired of. And an eclair with a cup of coffee really is delicious, something I can vouch for because they invited me to join them. As a general practitioner, I couldn't say no – it's something I want to make time for. It helps you to see your patients in a new light and they often tell you things they wouldn't say during a regular home visit. And the wonderful stories come for free. It's one of the lovely things about being a doctor. You get to know your patients even better."

Being present and sharing grief

"Mangomoments aren't necessarily happy moments. Sometimes they can run very deep. During kidney dialysis, an 86-year-old patient suffered a haematoma involving a dangerous blood clot. She wanted to undergo surgery. Her family didn't know what to do, as the operation was not without risk – a fact that the patient herself was well aware of. I spoke to the family and they finally made the difficult decision to respect the woman's wishes. Sadly, the operation was not a success, and the woman was put into an artificial coma and died the next day. I went with the family to see her in intensive care – it was a very profound and intense experience and we had a good conversation. We had a cup of coffee together, something I felt the family needed at that moment. It is important for people to be able to frame this type of experience and that's something that you, as a caregiver, can help with. Sometimes just by being present, saying goodbye together and sharing in the sadness. We have to make time for this. That human contact is so important.

It used to be the norm for general practitioners to visit their patients in hospital. Nowadays, this is becoming less common. Our diaries are full and social contact between people is less intense. Yet these visits are still valuable. Older people, in particular, who are in hospital after an operation often do not know exactly what happened and how long their rehabilitation will take. Caregivers need to make the time for this. It's always nice for patients to see a familiar face. It gives them confidence. People brighten up when you stop by, perhaps even with a small gift. I'd appreciate this myself if I were a patient. Ultimately, it only takes a bit of effort to visit patients you have known for years when they are in hospital or a residential care centre."

© Rob Stevens

VEERLE

MANGO *moment*

MANGO moment

ALL THE LATEST GOSSIP

"I'm Veerle and I became ill with lymphoma when I was twenty-seven. I've been undergoing treatment for almost four years now: light chemo, heavy chemo, radiation and two stem cell transplants. Once I was in isolation for three weeks. I've been in hospital a lot over the years, but an isolation ward is something else. You aren't allowed to leave your room and everyone who comes in is specially dressed and wears a mask over their mouth. It's a very antisocial environment. And everybody is always asking how you are. The doctor will come and examine you and check all your parameters, as will the nurses, physiotherapists and dieticians. All the caregivers are constantly busy with medical matters. Of course, completely understandable, but you don't get many other visitors, and visiting is limited anyway during isolation. Only my parents and my sister came by regularly. But they were so worried that they were constantly asking me about my medical condition as well. How are you? How are you feeling? Normal life passed me by completely. I existed only as a patient. That's how I felt. I was literally and metaphorically isolated."

I want you to have a good moan

"During that period, the logistics staff and the cleaning staff made a big difference to me. They came in and talked to each other and to me. About the usual things, all the latest gossip, or their minor everyday frustrations. These conversations made me feel like I was back in the land of the living and gave me a sense of life outside the hospital walls. They took my mind off cancer and blood counts for a moment and their chat distracted me and gave me a chance to laugh. They made me feel so good. Those staff members also brought in cards from friends and acquaintances and hung them up. They didn't dwell on my medical condition at all. What a relief! What a breath of fresh air! What the clinic clowns are for children, the cleaning and logistics staff were to me, as an adult. Those five or ten minutes a day, that was a Mangomoment every time. A laugh, a chat, simple as that.

People often don't know how to respond to someone who's ill. I felt my friends were trying their best not to whinge when they were around me. As if their problems were nothing compared to mine. Until one beautiful day I asked them to have a good moan to me. Their lives couldn't be perfect, after all. As soon as they started to confide in me about their own concerns, I felt much better. I had the same feeling as with the cleaning staff: they just told me what happened to them that day, without constantly reminding me of my illness. It made me feel like a human being rather than just a patient.

On days when I was feeling really ill, those employees automatically took that into account. They just went about their work quietly without saying anything. They are really good with people. I never actually thanked them for that. I should have, because they deserve it. They probably don't realise how much of a difference they made to me, and probably to other patients as well."

The impact of words

"Of course, the opposite happens from time to time, too. I remember an intake interview with a nurse. Trying to be positive, I said: 'In a year's time, I'm sure I'll be able to laugh at this.' But the nurse replied that I shouldn't be under any illusions, and that it would take much longer than that. That was on the first day, when I still had to get my stem cells. It brought me back down to earth with a bump. The nurse probably meant well, but people sometimes don't give very much thought to the effect their words might have.

On the other hand, there are lots of nice little touches. In the isolation ward they come round with the sweets trolley every day so you can choose something. That's a wow moment. There's also a treadmill for those who are allowed out of their room. It's really nice to know that people are constantly thinking about how to make patients' lives a little more enjoyable.

What I missed most at the hospital was a green space, a garden or a park. The year after my transplant, in 2014, I was admitted twelve times for infections. I was so pleased when my mum took me out in the wheelchair for five or ten minutes. When you're in hospital, you're stuck between the same four walls. I wanted to go outside and hear the birds singing. A garden or some greenery would do wonders for me."

The little things that you remember

"I still have a positive view of the healthcare system. After all, they cured me. They saved my life. I'm a nurse myself. I know how hard everyone is trying. I'm always involved in all decisions. The medical specialist was very open to this – perhaps because of my training. She even gave me her mobile number so I could call over the weekend for my results. That's when you feel a close bond. All things considered, it was a small gesture, but it's something I will never forget. It's a sign of trust.

At the end of the day, it's the little things you remember, and your family and friends play a role, too. My mum brought me a present every week. Often, they were silly little things: a pair of socks because I had cold feet on the hospital bed. But they were nicely wrapped and there was always that moment of surprise when I opened the package. I thought it was great.

As the hundredth day after my stem cell transplant approached – an important milestone for a good recovery – my friends had made a gift pack for the last ten days, from day ninety to day one hundred. I was allowed to open a gift every day. These were always small things: cardboard pots for ice cream, for example. But that was enough to put a smile on my face. At a time like this, you don't have the energy to do big things. A city break to New York would have been wonderful too, but I would never have been able to do that. I had to be so careful with immunity that I was actually locked up. I wasn't allowed to take a bus or train or go to the supermarket because there were too many people there. But I could go to the park. Great! Some time in nature. It's the little things that count. Nowadays I make a conscious effort to volunteer. I read the paper to an elderly gentleman who's going blind. Or I spend an afternoon knitting or reading with an elderly lady whose daughter, who used to take care of her, now has breast cancer. It makes me very happy to be able to do things like that for people."

MIRRE MANGO *moment*

THOSE MOMENTS MAKE MY JOB AS A DOCTOR SO MUCH MORE ENJOYABLE

MANGO moment

"I'm Mirre, a surgeon specialising in oncology and gastroenterology. I often stand beside my patients in the operating theatre while they are waiting to 'go under' – this can be a scary moment and they need reassurance. As a doctor, you can give them that just by being there, by putting a hand on their shoulder or chatting to them. For example, I had a lovely conversation with a woman about nature. She told me about going for walks in the woods and talked about things like chestnuts. Ever since, she has given me a bag of chestnuts every year. This was clearly a Mangomoment for her, but now I get one, too, year in, year out.

Being thoughtful, showing compassion – I don't think it's happening enough yet. These things seem like the most normal thing in the world to me, but when I look around me, I think we could all do even more along these lines. Of course, our high workload, interrelationships and administrative burden mean that this is not always easy. But I always try to think, 'Imagine if that was you lying there. What would you want if you were the patient? What would you need?' Patients suffer from a great deal of uncertainty and anxiety. Doctors and other caregivers can alleviate these fears by a small gesture, a little extra attention, a kind word. Patients feel very dependent. That's not a good feeling."

A world of difference

"Caregivers need to be sensitive to this, and of course I'm talking about doctors as well as nurses here. Once you have experienced what it's like to be a patient for yourself, you become more aware of what really matters at moments like this. For example, the period after a test when you are waiting for the result is always a particularly tense time for patients. They might be worrying whether they have cancer. Not knowing, whilst being aware that tests are being done, or may even have been completed, makes it very difficult to wait. We need to respond better to that. Once the patient's results are in, I think we should notify them as soon as possible. Even if they have an appointment in three days' time, why leave them in fear and uncertainty for another three days and nights? Just calling and giving them the good news makes a world of difference.

There's a cultural shift going on. I can feel it around me. Mangomoments matter more than ever. We must strive for a chain of Mangomoments, a series of sincere and authentic acts of attention for every patient, for every human being. Organisations can be part of this too. Satisfied staff mean satisfied patients, so that's where it all starts. If organisations pay their employees some attention, employees will pass this on to their patients: the one thing is not separate from the other. Self-care, courtesy for each other, a good atmosphere – these are what allow Mangomoments to flourish. If there is an open culture with room for creativity and innovation, but also for feedback, there will also be more room for the human being behind the employee. This also makes it easier to train and coach people, and to set a good example. It's all about training entire teams instead of individuals. Because in the end we need to achieve a culture of hospitality and accountability amongst the staff. And that's something you can create. It's a question of mirroring: what you give out you tend to get back. A culture of openness, friendliness and good feedback makes all the difference.

Mangomoments are all around us. The essence is a smile, a friendly gesture. It all starts on the phone, with the patient's first contact with us. That's where their care experience begins. The staff who meet the patient first have an important role to play. Patients and their families are often a little nervous when they arrive at the hospital. They feel small and insecure. A smile can be very reassuring, which is exactly what people need. It takes no effort and no time, just a bit of attention. Just looking at people in a friendly way can make all the difference."

You get back what you give out

"We need to embed the culture of Mangomoments into our organisations across the board. Mangomoments need to become mango years. Isn't it strange that we're so happy about a Mangomoment? Isn't that a sign that there's a lot of work to be done? We not only need to provide good care in a technical sense, we also need to provide care that is warm-hearted and human. Becoming aware of this is an important first step.

Accountability is just as important. People need to know they can count on you. It inspires so much confidence. Everyone in the organisation needs to be accountable – from secretaries to nurses and doctors. If you agree something with a patient, make sure you follow through on it. Sadly, we often fall short in this area. Maybe we promised to call a patient this afternoon, but we asked a colleague to do it for us and they didn't know it was supposed to be today – that sort of thing. Again, waiting for results has a huge impact on patients. Every caregiver involved must be aware of, and live up to, their responsibility. This is another aspect of Mangomoments: saying what you will do and doing what you have said you will.

I have spent a long time in hospital myself. It's often the nurses you are closest to, but doctors can also have very intense moments with a patient. Doctors who are open to this and give it some thought can very easily give their patients Mangomoments. It's all about compassion. Authentic attention. As a doctor, this is something that energises me, by the way. Those little gestures that make a difference to the patient also make my job much more enjoyable."

THE MANGOMOMENT OF CHAHRAZAD

MANGO moment

MANGO moment

KINDNESS IS THE MAGIC WORD

"My grandma had had a fall. In the emergency room we were told that her hip was broken and she needed an operation. But, in the end, she had a number of complications and had to stay in hospital for more than three weeks after this. She was even in intensive care for a while. That was where we had a Mangomoment to remember.

Grandma is illiterate and doesn't know a word of the local language as she only speaks Arabic. In Arabic, we call her Yemma. When we, the grandchildren, are around, we can interpret for her. But there's another problem. My grandmother has dementia and she often forgets what's going on and who the people around her are. This sometimes makes her panic and, of course, we – her family – worry about this all the time. How will things go with grandma? Is she able to make herself understood? Does she understand what's happening? Is she panicking? It's hard for us to leave Grandma alone, because she doesn't know what's going on and that upsets her. It's not nice for the caregivers either."

Words above the bed

"Grandma had been admitted into hospital before. Back then, we tried to arrange for one family member to stay with her at all times, even at night. This worked pretty well, but it wasn't possible when she was in intensive care. We were talking this over with a friendly nurse when, between us, we came up with the idea of writing down some important Arabic words phonetically. Very simple things like 'hello', 'food', 'water', 'sleep', 'is everything okay?', etc. We hung those words above Grandma's bed, so that every caregiver could see and use them. And they did. It was fantastic. We were incredibly reassured by the fact that caregivers were making an effort to communicate with grandma. No matter how difficult it was at times, they were able to make contact. My grandmother also noticed that the caregivers were making the effort and that alone reassured her. It's a friendly gesture when someone tries to speak to you in your own language. It inspires confidence if someone is doing their best to do that.

I remember that nurse very well, even now. He was a very friendly man, always ready to help. He knew we were worried and came over and gave us an update every time we came to visit. Thanks to his good care, and that of his colleagues, my grandmother was much less panicked by the tubes on her body and the machines that surrounded her. There was always someone around to reassure her when this was needed. When we came to visit, the caregivers would tell us which words Grandma had used, and ask what they meant. They really did their best to make sure communication was as good, and as personal, as possible.

You can't imagine how much it meant to the whole family, just to know that grandma was in good hands. This is particularly important in intensive care. The situation is so serious and visiting hours are limited. But if caregivers show that they are making an effort, it reassures us. We had an agreement with the nurse that he would call us straight away if anything serious was going on. We knew we could trust him. That gave us a lot of peace of mind."

Good vibes inspire confidence

"Most caregivers were very cooperative, but not all of them. Not that they were unkind, but it was clear that some of them didn't know how to deal with my grandma's situation. Other staff were very friendly. They made time for my grandma, and for us, even during busy periods. They were always patient, always kind, and did everything with a smile.

These efforts had a positive effect on my grandma. She was less restless and less panicky, which also made her a calmer and easier patient. Kindness is the magic word.

When grandma was moved onto an ordinary ward, the words on paper went with her. There, too, there were caregivers who went along with this enthusiastically. This created a good vibe and a sense of trust that spread to my grandma. Even if she didn't understand what the nurse was saying, a friendly gesture and a smile speak volumes. Non-verbal communication is even more important than words on paper. But, here too, it's the gesture that counts. A gesture of approachability and openness.

If caregivers take their time and show patience, it's good for everyone. First and foremost for the patient and their family, but also for the caregiver and for the organisation as a whole. Happy patients are grateful and they show it. We explicitly thanked the nurses for their efforts, for the trust they inspired and for making us feel good. I hope that other teams in other wards pick up on these things. In any case, our family will choose that hospital again in the future if any of us are in need of care. Because we know we're welcome and because we have faith in the people who work there."

VÉRONIQUE

MANGO moment

MANGO moment

THE NEED FOR COSY LIGHT

"One Mangomoment I think about a lot concerns a woman with uterine cancer I treated as a gynaecologist. Her cancer was at an advanced stage. One day I had a profound conversation with her. It was her that brought the subject up: she knew her illness was untreatable and felt that the end was coming. We talked about death, about saying goodbye and how she felt about it.

The next day, I thought about that conversation a lot. I went to see the woman again to find out how she was feeling. She said she wasn't afraid of dying, but she was afraid of how it would happen. She couldn't imagine death. But when she was lying there in the dark, she saw all kinds of forms and figures, as children sometimes do, and that made her anxious and restless.

I suggested leaving the light on in the room at night, but she said she found the hospital light too sad and gloomy. She talked about her floor lamp at home and the pleasant, cosy light it gave out. I sensed that she wanted her lamp from home, but didn't dare to ask. Patients don't normally bring their own furniture to hospital with them, nor is it customary for doctors to discuss this with their patients. Still, I realised how important it was for her and suggested that she have her floor lamp picked up from home. And she was very happy about that."

Dispelling fear and uncertainty

"Over the next few days and nights she was much calmer and less anxious. The familiar light of her floor lamp drove away the figures that frightened her in the dark. As a caregiver, I felt good about that. When a small gesture has such a tremendous impact on how a person feels in the depths of their being and during their final days, it is a great pleasure. If you can dispel someone's fear and uncertainty about death and give that person peace of mind, then you have made a real difference.

As caregivers, we have to be open to that sort of thing. We need to be able to pick up on those signals. And we do have the instincts and senses to do this. It's why we choose to work in this field in the first place: we want to help vulnerable people. That's what drives us. But sometimes that motivation tails off a bit over time. Sometimes the environment makes it difficult to give our all. And sometimes we get a bit hardened and cynical. If there is too much control, measurement and management, you will end up with computer-controlled, emotionless care. That leaves a bad taste in the mouth. You know what you should be doing, but you aren't given a chance. That's dangerous, because it wears you down. As a caregiver, you need the right conditions to do your job as it should be done: with feeling and compassion, and with the whole person in mind."

Giving staff room to manoeuvre

"Every organisation not only needs to give its employees the space they need, it also needs to motivate them. Good care has to be fed from above. I'm well aware that those little things that make a difference also have a cost in terms of time, energy and resources. But in the long run they lead to better care. Culture is a big part of this, too. And it's an ethical issue. We need to focus not only on the patient, but also on the human being as a whole. That goes much further and deeper than just keeping an eye on the disease.

We need to pay attention to Mangomoments. Many doctors and other caregivers will recognise these stories and situations. It is good that we are having this conversation. People are often afraid to bring up the system. But if we can put this issue high on the agenda and involve a lot of people, we can open the subject up for discussion, both within organisations and across the sector as a whole.

Mangomoments need to be given every chance to flourish. That means that I, as a doctor, also have to make choices. Caregivers need to find the right balance. What can we do, and what can't we? Let's have a debate on that. This calls for honest and open communication. Especially as the care sector is short staffed in the first place. First do no harm. That's what we say. But it falls wide of the mark. We want to provide dignified care, not just carry out the right actions from a technical point of view. That is at the heart of the debate, and I know it's something that many doctors and caregivers think about a lot. We all want to provide warm, humane care. And those little things, like allowing a cosy lamp into a room, can work wonders."

© Manon Vanhaecht

MANGO moment

THE MANGOMOMENT OF **CHRISTIANE AND ANDRÉ**

MANGO moment

MULLED WINE IN THE SNOW

"That was a long time ago! All that snow that suddenly swirled from the sky, creating a beautiful snow carpet in no time. What a wonderful spectacle! I was walking through the corridors of the care home feeling very excited. Almost like being a kid again. It was partly because of all those beautiful memories that suddenly went through my head. Memories from my childhood and the years when Christiane and I used to go out walking in the snow together. How we used to enjoy it! The wintry atmosphere, the people, the conviviality and, of course, the glass of mulled wine.

Occupational therapist Isabelle saw me wandering down the halls with my head in the clouds. She realised straight away how excited I felt. She laughed at me and pointed to the snow that was still swirling joyously around the courtyard. 'Want to play outside?', she asked teasingly. 'Very much', I laughed back. I knew she was kidding, but I meant it. And somehow Isabelle noticed that. I saw her hesitate.

A little later Isabelle and Ruta knocked on the door of our room. 'Still in the mood for some fun in the snow?' 'Are you kidding? Definitely!' Christiane and I dressed warmly. Ruta helped us and even did Christiane's make up because she wanted to take our photo. Isabelle had fetched a bottle of mulled wine from the basement as an extra surprise. So we all went out together. In the snow. What a wonderful feeling! The cold air, the crisp snow under our feet, the flakes on our clothes and our faces ... Christiane and I instantly felt at least fifty years younger!

Soon, other residents came out as well, all wrapped up warm in jackets and scarves. I can see it in my mind's eye – all those wheelchairs and walkers in the fresh snow. Careful and exuberant at the same time. What a party!

The picture they took of Christiane and me was beautiful. Just the two of us in the snow with a glass of mulled wine. It looked so lovely the care home made it into a Christmas card! And proud we were, of course. But most of all, we were happy and grateful that we were still able to have such an experience! It brings us pleasure every time we think about it."

That sparkle in their eyes

For occupational therapist Isabelle and maintenance worker Ruta, too, it was a day to remember. "When it suddenly started to snow, you could sense that the residents were excited. Especially André! Everyone felt the child in them waking up and happy memories were brought back. All those soft, white flakes in the courtyard. I went outside to bring in some handfuls of snow for the residents to feel. But from the sparkle in their eyes, I could see that they wanted to go outside themselves. It was so beautiful. Of course, at first you think: no way. But that quickly turned into: well, why not? It just seemed so lovely", says Isabelle.

"First we took Christiane and André outside", says Ruta. "Other residents saw us and, of course, they wanted to go outside as well. Some even wanted to throw snowballs! In the end, we brought out a lot of residents, walking frames and wheelchairs included, quite a work. It turned into a great photo shoot. Activities like this bring back enthusiasm to our residents. It's an extra effort for the staff, but when it happens so spontaneously, it's really lovely. And it enables teamwork. We prepared everything together, made it happen and cleared everything up together afterwards. That's all part of it, of course.

If I were only allowed to do the things that are strictly within my remit, I wouldn't be as happy here as I am. The freedom to do that little bit more for people makes me enthusiastic about my job. As a maintenance worker, I feel like part of the team. I work with my colleagues to provide warm-hearted care."

Isabelle feels the same. "Every night, I want to feel good when I look back on the day. Every resident is different and every day is a surprise. Being able to respond to opportunities as they come up is a great thing. Residents still want to enjoy themselves, each in their own way. You can sense their needs and wishes. I'm happy to let planned activities go by the board if I can give the residents a treat by doing something else. Like when it snowed. That happens so rarely that you have to seize the moment when it's there. Residents and family members still talk about the photo shoot in the snow. That one Mangomoment keeps on resonating and warming hearts long after the snow has melted. Beautiful, isn't it?"

© Rob Stevens

MANGO moment MARJOLEIN

MANGO moment

THIS GOES RIGHT TO THE HEART OF GOOD CARE

"As a nurse, I can think of dozens of examples of Mangomoments. Nothing spectacular, but essential nonetheless. Recently, for example, there was a woman who came onto my ward after a few weeks in intensive care. When I first met her on a Saturday morning, she looked washed out and exhausted. She was in an extremely weakened state physically, but also mentally at the end of her strength. She could no longer eat without assistance. She needed blood infusions. She didn't care about anything anymore. She just couldn't be bothered. Because of the complications she'd had over the past few weeks she had lost confidence in her own body and that led to a loss of confidence in her future. She didn't have even a glimmer of hope. Or, rather, there was just one glimmer left. That was her faith. Somewhere deep down, she believed that God wouldn't let her down. That's where she drew her last strength from."

Moved to tears

"When she told me this openly and sincerely, I asked her if she would like to attend the Eucharist. She thought it was impossible. She was too weak and, besides, she was stuck with all those infusions. I told her that I could take her bed to the hospital chapel, where there was a mass that Sunday. She hesitated for a moment, but she thought it was a great idea. So, the next day I went into the hospital extra early to do her make-up, so she would feel better about herself. When it was time for mass, I took her over there, bed and all, plus everything attached to it. A volunteer took over from me there. I was on standby in case I was needed.

After the mass, I went to pick her up. She was moved to tears because she had been able to reconnect with her faith. The mass had given her the strength to resume her recovery. You can safely say that that was a turning point in her healing.

Those moments are what you do it for. In the end, I didn't do much. But for that woman it was like a bright spot from which she drew strength to cope with her illness. My role was actually minimal and basic. But, for me, this goes straight to the heart of good care. That's what it's all about."

Setting a good example for each other

"Total focus on the human being behind the patient. Caregivers who get this right have a major effect not only on the patient, but also on themselves too. It's such a good feeling! It's the reason I, and so many others, went into this profession in the first place. I want to mean something to another human being. With workloads as they are, this is not always self-evident. If you don't have much time, you focus primarily on the technical things because you have to get them done. I don't like it when there's no time for the human being behind the patient. That's not what I want. That's why the concept of Mangomoments has caught on the way it has. It reminds us of our deepest inner motivation.

An effective nurse is one that has not only mastered the technical procedures, but is also good with people and has compassion. My colleagues and I are sincerely moved when we watch the original clip from the documentary featuring Viviane and Annemie. Anyone who works in the healthcare sector will recognise this. Along with our organisation, we took part in the 'What matters to you?' day. This concept fits in well with the idea of Mangomoments.

It's all about authentic and valuable attention for the human being behind the patient. We are going to pick this up and run with it. We have challenged all our colleagues to share their most beautiful Mangomoments with each other. That creates so much energy! It empowers people and it opens things up for discussion. It's lovely.

For me, Mangomoments are the very essence of care. They are what it's all about. A patient does not deserve 'extra attention'; this should be part of their normal, day-to-day care. Every day has its goosebumps moment when you keep the human being behind the patient in view. Pressure of work and the tight labour market mean that Mangomoments are not always self-evident. But they should be. Because they go right to the heart of good care."

© Rob Stevens

PHILIPPE MANGO moment

MANGO moment

LOOK THEM IN THE EYE BEFORE YOU LOOK IN THEIR MOUTHS

"I was referred to a large hospital with a tumour in my sinus cavity. The local hospital hadn't been able to help me, but neither did it fill me with confidence. The doctor there was sitting behind his computer screen and barely looked up when I came in. The welcome I received at the second hospital couldn't have been more different. The night before my operation, the doctor stopped by to see me, saying 'you'll heal quickly'. I looked at him questioningly. 'Optimists heal faster. I can't prove it, and there's no scientific research on the subject, but that's what I see happening.' I liked that and I thanked him for it. The next day, he operated on me. In the weeks that followed, I was mainly in contact with other doctors on his team.

One Friday morning, a few weeks later, he suddenly called me at home, apologising for not being in touch sooner. I found it remarkable that he took the trouble to call, and that he apologised. He then explained what was going on and what the complications were. He was very well informed, which isn't as self-evident as it seems, because in a training hospital it is often junior doctors who take care of the follow-up. I thought it was great that he paid me that courtesy and it made me very happy. I told him and he seemed a little surprised. 'That's my job', he said."

Can I have a hug?

"I won't forget the contact I have had with my dentist, either. She made the dental prosthesis I needed after my surgery and I had to go and see her around forty times. She makes paying people positive attention seem like the most natural thing in the world. She does this not only with her patients, but also with colleagues, administrative staff and students. At one point, I asked if I could give her a hug. She agreed. It was an intensely human moment. Of course, you also have to be able to remain critical of each other. Because that can be a pitfall. But that has never been a problem for me.

A good understanding between doctor and patient can do so much good in a care relationship. I am convinced that the number of complaints and medical errors would fall dramatically if patients and doctors could talk about risks and choices in an open and adult way.

Often, it is the little things that create a personal connection. Two years after my surgery, I was in the hospital with my wife when I spotted a surgeon who treated me at the end of the corridor. I gave him a wave. He recognised me, broke off the conversation with his colleagues and rushed over to greet my wife and me. He was so full of empathy! He showed genuine interest in how my wife was doing, too, because this was not an easy period for her either. I was moved by his interest.

The contrast with that uninterested doctor I met earlier could hardly be greater. I had the same experience with my dentist. She immediately connected with me as a human being. She always looks me in the eye before she looks in my mouth. That's what it's all about."

I can do without my lunch break if I have to

The surgeon who treated Philippe about his role: "I often get feedback from patients, sometimes in words and sometimes in body language. It's no coincidence that I greeted Philippe and his wife in the hospital corridor. I know those little things add something essential to the care relationship. I do it quite deliberately. It's not that I have to because, at the end of the day, it's none of my business how things are going at home. But I know that it is important for patients and their families to feel that I have empathy for them. I also know that this changes how patients see our team in the hospital. It means they start to see us as people who are concerned about their care as a whole and about the entire human being. In other words, it creates a different relationship.

If patients feel that you're interested and that you're on their side, they'll be quicker to ask a question the next time they need to; they won't wait so long before they raise a subject. This improves the quality of care. Taking time for people is so important. And you have to make that time. If necessary, you have to manage without your lunch break, or make the next patient wait a little longer. Then, when I start the next consultation, I apologise for the wait. That's what I learned during my training.

I try to pass this on to my assistants, too. The importance of body language, for example. If I notice any signs of fear or pain, I point them out to my assistants so they learn to spot them too. I also pay attention to the body language of junior doctors during patient consultations and I give feedback if necessary. Doctors and other caregivers should not only be able to read body language, they should also be constantly aware of the signals they themselves are giving out.

For example, when I visit a patient's room I often sit down for a moment to talk. It sends the patient a signal that I am making time for them. Even if the conversation only lasts five minutes, it still feels very different to the patient than if I were to stand in the doorway. Having a conversation while seated also reduces the distance between patient and doctor. All those things make a difference."

First in the eyes, then in the mouth

The dentist who treated Philippe was also happy to talk about the way she sees things: "Look your patient in the eyes before you look in their mouth. That's something that I always impress upon my students. First, look who's in front of you. What are the patient's expectations? How are they feeling? Are they scared? Hopeful? Nervous? Anything a patient says, whether in words or by their body language, can help you work together to find the right solution. In our field, there is often more than one treatment option. The most appropriate solution will vary from person to person and we work this out by talking to the patient. So you really do need to make a connection. Besides, when it's me that needs treatment, I always like to be seen first and foremost as a human being and only then as someone with pain in their finger.

Philippe wasn't your average patient. From a technical point of view, it was a very difficult process – we were doing something we'd never done before. We spent hours together, sometimes until late at night. But I notice this need for security with other patients, too. It may sound like a bit of a cliché, but patients appreciate it if you make them feel as if they are being taken care of.

Of course, that can take time and students and colleagues sometimes point this out, commenting that I spend a lot of time talking to patients. But I think it makes a difference in the quality of care. And sometimes you save a lot of time by listening carefully to people. And that leaves them more satisfied with the end result."

Not an easy message, but an essential one

"I also try to be very honest. 'Things will never be the way they were before.' That's not an easy message, but it's an essential one. And you have to listen carefully and show the patient that you understand that it is difficult for them to deal with that reality. That understanding makes acceptance easier. Make sure patients can tell you their story. That's so important.

Always try to give the patient your full attention. You have to be in the moment, listen openly, don't get too involved and definitely don't jump to conclusions. If you manage to do that you will build trust. And that's where everything starts.

I'm making it sound as if I always do everything perfectly, but of course I don't. Sometimes I have to give in to time pressure. And, it's just harder to build a good relationship with some patients than with others. Even so, I always try to create an environment where people can tell their story.

Creating a Mangomoment is no trouble, it's something I really enjoy doing. It gives me so much satisfaction; I get so much back from it. You wouldn't believe how much energy patients give me.

That's the message I pass onto my students: first and foremost, provide care. As a doctor, there are many important things you have to do but, above all, you have to provide care. It feels so worthwhile. You should bear in mind how much it can mean to someone if you are able to provide care for them. Do it with all your heart. Why else would we do this job? Just for the money? That's not what it's all about, is it?

It's in so many little things. When I'm doing something technical that takes more than fifteen minutes, I ask the patient which radio station they prefer to listen to – and then I put that station on and try to remember it for next time. People like that, and they show it.

Sometimes I put my hand on a patient's shoulder briefly during treatment and ask if they are still okay. By doing that I show that I'm thinking about them.

I can't prove it, but I'm convinced that those little gestures, those Mangomoments, make a difference to the healing process. If you get people involved and make them feel good, their recovery will be easier. Positivity works."

LISA MANGO moment

MANGO moment

SEE THE OPPORTUNITIES AND GRAB THEM

"I have had an independent practice as a speech therapist since 2016. One of my patients was a lady who had always led a busy and varied life. She'd travelled a lot, been on stage and given lectures. But suddenly, an autoimmune muscle disease put a stop to all this, leaving her barely able to speak or swallow. She came to see me to practice those skills.

When we first met, I asked her about things she'd like to be able to do again. The answer was surprising and disarming. 'I'd really like to act again. I know it's going to be hard, but it has made me so happy. It's my joy and my life.' She was so passionate that I built all her therapy sessions around theatre and performance. We were constantly working with theatre scripts. She loved it. Her illness had made her feel excluded from her familiar environment; she couldn't take part in it anymore, and her social life had suffered, too. But working on plays again got her back into readings and theatre."

Yes, I was proud

"Thanks to new medication, the woman gradually regained her vocal power. She continued to make progress and was able to realise her dream of being back on stage. She got a part in a play and when it was being performed, she sent me an invitation. It was as if she wanted to tell me 'we did this together and it worked'. The impact on the quality of her life was enormous. And, of course, I enjoyed it. Yes, I was proud to see her on that stage. More than a year later she sent me an audio clip so I could hear the progress she had made since then. She kept on practicing, even after the therapy had finished. It was lovely to hear that she was doing well and that she was still thinking about our sessions. At moments like that, you feel that you really mean something to someone.

Actually, it didn't take much effort to adapt the scripts for that woman rather than using the standard texts from a handbook. I've often noticed that it gives patients a boost if they can see that you are making an extra effort yourself. Because you're trying to adapt to what interests them. That's why I always ask about someone's passions or interests. Patients like that. It makes the therapy less boring, and more recognisable. It can also be an opportunity to get to know each other better. To build trust. They say something about their interests, I say something about myself. If you have a connection with someone, you're both more motivated to do your best."

What motivates me

"You won't make that connection with everyone. It has to be something that comes from both of you – the patient has to allow it. And, sometimes, you just don't click with each other. But I do try, because it makes my work more interesting and more enjoyable. It's what keeps me motivated, day in day out.

I have also done a lot of volunteering with palliative patients and with elderly people who are ill, sometimes staying overnight or keeping them company. You get to know people quickly when you do that. I started volunteering because my grandfather's brother was completely alone when he died and I thought that was terrible. I want to bring people out of their isolation. That's part of what motivates me in my job.

The more I think about it, the more convinced I become that, as a caregiver, you have to create the space for Mangomoments yourself. Ultimately, it's all about personal care that keeps the individual patient in view. As a caregiver, you have to be open to Mangomoments. There are always plenty of opportunities, but you have to see them and grab them."

© Kim van den Adel

NIEK MANGO moment

MANGO moment

TEN EUROS POORER, BUT I'VE GAINED A GOOD MOOD

"When I wake up feeling broken, I always go and fill up at Ali's. Even if I don't actually need to – I'll even make a detour to get there. But I'm happy to do that. Those are the mornings after a gruelling night when pain has won out over the need for sleep. That happens all too often since my motorbike accident. And, in the morning, I feel like a wreck. I take a seat in the shower chair and try to wash away my anger and sadness and then climb into the car with my assistance dog Joep and head off to Ali's.

I don't know if it's me or my van that he recognises, but Ali always gives me a cheerful wave when I flash my lights. He's always there, by the way – I think he must work day and night. I turn off my engine, open the window and Ali comes over with a smile on his face. 'Whatcha, pal!' (For those that don't know, round here calling someone 'pal' means they're your mate). 'Fill her up?' I nod. Ali carefully opens the door. Carefully, because he once got his hand trapped in the heavy door of my van and couldn't work for weeks. Something he's never blamed me for, by the way.

'What do you do for a living, anyway?', Ali asks. 'Today I'm going to work undercover in an organisation.' He looks alarmed and stops filling up. 'Are you a cop, then?', he asks. I understand his suspicion right away. Ali once told me this was his first real job. He was in prison for years and his experience with the police has not been good. 'No, I'm not', I reassure him. 'I'm going undercover today as a nurse.' Ali seems relieved and carries on filling up. 'Hey, that's only five litres!' he exclaims. 'That's possible. I only came because I wanted cheering up.'

'Are you in pain again? I could see you were. You know, when I'm in pain, I always pinch my arm so hard that it blocks out the other pain. That helps.' Ali has a solution for everything.

'How long have you been in that wheelchair?' he asks. 'Five years now', I answer. Well, I'd get a different doctor if I were you', he says grinning from ear to ear. I laugh too. As it happens, Ali also has a cousin who can help me with my spinal cord injury. Yes, Ali's got a solution for everything.

'You know what: I'll make you a nice cup of coffee.' A little later he checks my tyres. Or, at any rate, he kicks them. I give him my cash card and the pin number. 'Hey, dude, be careful who you give that to!' he laughs. He comes back and gives me another can of pop. 'Take care, mate. 'And come back and fill up again soon.'

I drive away. Ten euros poorer, but I've gained a good mood."

No time? Make time!

"Don't we all have the choice of being a bit more like Ali from time to time? Even if the electronic patient record is not cooperating, the consultation time is up or the ward is understaffed yet again. Even so, there is always an opportunity to brighten up someone's day a bit. You could call them Ali moments; you could call them Mangomoments. I have experienced dozens of these beautiful moments for myself.

Years ago, for example, I was in a rehabilitation centre on a ward with six patients. One by one, the other patients were allowed to return home. But I was in a worse state than any of them, and had to stay where I was. It was really starting to get me down, and caregiver Jannie noticed. One Saturday night, she came to see me unexpectedly. She had made me brie on toast. It was an unforgettable moment. What I needed was for someone to just put an arm around me. In the hustle and bustle of daily care, this doesn't always happen.

Sometimes I think caregivers should take the time to do that more often. Even if there isn't time, you can make time. Because getting more time just isn't going to happen. Making time for a patient is part of good care, isn't it? Isn't that the main reason caregivers chose this profession in the first place? Isn't that the intrinsic motivation that makes not only patients, but also the caregivers themselves, feel a lot better after a Mangomoment?"

MANGO moment VANIA

MANGO moment

LEADERSHIP FROM THE HEART

"I am a dancer, choreographer, and activist for cultural change, fighting for hospitals to treat humans as individuals who benefit from having access to creative and expressive arts during hospitalisation. I am the founder of Dancin Power. My life has had its fair share of both successes and setbacks; nevertheless, despite the struggles and hardship, I have learned from my grandmother Alzira to not miss the beauty of Mangomoments. Well, she didn't use that term back then, but you get the idea. She did teach me to pause, observe, and appreciate every experience I've had in my life. She believed that everything we go through, the happy and sad moments, both come to teach us a lesson.

I was born in Rio de Janeiro-Brazil, in one of the poorest and most dangerous corners of the entire state. Our family moved from the city to another state, Minas Gerais, to escape the terrifying violence in our neighbourhood, and we made a home for ourselves in a remote, isolated area with no running water or electricity, where we walked for four hours each day to get to school. At the age of ten, I endured significant childhood trauma that left me with severe PTSD. At eighteen, I became, with both joy and fear, a single mother. In the face of these and many other challenges, music and dance provided the outlet I needed to cope with my emotions and fears and find healing. I grew up with the dream to be able to one day use the power of music and dance to help other children facing trauma, just like it helped me when I needed it. I had no idea how I would ever do that, or when, I just had that dream in my heart.

Thanks to dance, and the love and care of my strong and resilient grandmother, Alzira, I kept going, doing my best to build a life for my son and me. After losing my job and not being able to provide for my son, I moved to the United States in search of my version of the American Dream. I wanted to earn enough to provide for my son and my family back in Brazil, and one day, to bring my only child to the United States, so that he could have a chance to pursue higher education, and have opportunities for a better life.

Little did I know, the reality of life in the United States was not at all what I remembered seeing in the movies while living in Brazil. In fact, it was far from what I imagined it to be. Once I arrived in California, I started to work at three jobs, starting at 5:45 am at a coffee shop as a barista, and ending my workdays at 12:00 am as a restaurant hostess. At that time, I had to endure that daily routine so that I could afford my rent, food, and the money I sent back home to support my son and family in Brazil every month."

A life-call ringing

"After two years with somewhat English proficiency, thanks to the immersion, I was able to secure a job at the Oakland Public School System as a performing arts teacher. Remember that dream I had to one day be able to use dance to help others? Yes, I thought that by becoming a dance teacher in East Oakland, a place similar to the Baixada Fluminense in Rio de Janeiro, the place I grew up, I would maybe be fulfilling that dream. The job at the school was gratifying, and transformative, as I saw the positive impact the curriculum I developed had on the youth, but still, that wasn't it.

Then, one day, as I was biking from one public school to another to teach, I stopped at a red light in front of the Children's Hospital Oakland, and that was it, that very moment I felt something I had never felt before. As I looked up at the windows, my heart started to pound, it almost felt like I was losing my breath, which made me stop biking, and move to the sidewalk. At that moment I knew what was happening, my life calling was ringing, and I needed to answer. I felt in my heart the need to bring dance to the lives of the children who were hospitalised. Those children in hospital rooms often feel trapped, depressed, and terrified, hooked to IVs and kept secluded from their school, friends, and family. I immediately identified with the kids. I then thought: How wonderful it will be to be able to share my passion for music and dance to help these hospitalised children who, like I did, find themselves in a situation they never asked for; they could absolutely benefit from the magic and power music, dance, and mindfulness bring to someone's life.

With an enormous dose of enthusiasm, I approached the hospital with my idea. And of course, I ended up receiving a clean and kind 'No, thank you, we do not believe a hospital is a place for kids to dance'. Hearing that made me feel disappointed and sad, but not so sad to discourage me into giving up. I proceeded to contact the volunteer services, again and again, hoping I would get someone else on the phone, who would be open to the idea I was presenting.

After months trying, and many other 'No thank you's from the hospital's volunteer services, I realised that I needed to make a change of plans. The hospital by then had gotten very good in sending me rejections in the course of the long eight months. What they didn't know was that I had willpower made out of titanium, thanks to the many adversities and struggles I have in my life.

That is when I decided to apply for an entry-level position, which I landed as a registration associate at the ER in the admissions department. I was hired on March 13, 2006, and in less than two weeks, I was able to go around the hospital and find the key person I'd need to speak with to get permission to teach uplifting dance lessons to the patients. I pitched my idea to Maggie, the child life specialist and school room coordinator, and despite being very skeptical of the concept, she allowed me to give it a try. We discussed the safety guidelines, and I reassured her that I had already thought about that, and would keep safety as my priority; the dance moves would be adjusted to meet the kids where they were, physically and emotionally. She did tell me that since dance had never been offered at the hospital, kids might not be open to it, so she highly recommended that I don't take the lack of patient participation personally. The next day, during my lunch hour, I put on some colorful dance clothes, grabbed the boombox I had gotten from a friend as a gift to use at the hospital, and walked up the fourth floor to teach my very first adapted dance lesson. The session was a success, bringing joy to the lives of patients, their caregivers, and hospital staff. From that day on, I never stopped teaching."

A little kindness can go a long way

"Today, over thirteen years later, my life calling has become my life's work. Despite being someone who came to the United States as an immigrant with $20 in her pocket and without speaking English, I founded Dancin Power[1], a nonprofit organisation that uses the power of music, mindfulness, and dance to improve hospitalised children's lives.

I am beyond grateful to say it out loud and proud how beautiful it is that something that started so small, inside my heart, has now grown to impact so many lives. To me, that is a clear proof that everyone can make a difference in someone's life, no matter how small the gesture is, a little kindness can go a long way.

By leading from the heart, a successful teaching training program was developed that has trained over ninety artists using Dancin Power's methodology and approach. And most importantly, the lives of over 18,941 hospitalized children and their families have been positively impacted."

Memories to hold onto

"When I think about the past thirteen years, and all the Mangomoments I was honored to witness, the most touching one happened one morning at the pediatric hospice we serve, George Mark Children's House. That session included a 16-year-old girl at the end of her life, her Spanish-speaking father, her aunt, and some staff members.

She was very interested in the music and dancing, but was only able to move her arms and hands while lying in her bed. To encourage her to continue her 'special dancing', and to include family in the session, the Dancin Power leader suggested to dad that he and his sister participate as well. Dad was reluctant at first; however, his daughter was very interested in seeing him dance with his sister. Slowly he began to move his arms and feet, then his sister began to move, and as the music continued, they started dancing faster and faster, smiling and laughing, with his daughter grinning and laughing, all of them forgetting for that brief time, the seriousness of their situation. The patient and her family, utterly joyful as they shared these special moments, moments that would, in the next few months, become memories that the dad could hold onto after his daughter died.

The pediatric hospice made a bereavement follow-up call to this family and the dad, without prompting and without hesitation, talked to the social worker about their dancing session. He said he had not seen his daughter laugh like that in quite a long time, and he realised that he had not laughed like that since she had become ill, and how uplifting, joyful, and unforgettable it had felt to share that experience with her."

As Patti Maloney, Master of Social Work at George Mark Children's House puts it: "Dancin Power not only helped this family while the patient was alive, but they also gave this father beautiful memories to hold onto after he was no longer able to hold onto his daughter."

"I must say, thanks to bravery, resilience, perseverance of everyone involved in the daily care of the patients, and of course, the incredible group of Dancin Power teachers serving children's hospitals across the United States, we have been able to create more than 18,941 Mangomoments!"

1 www.dancinpower.org

THE MANGOMOMENT MODEL

Kris Vanhaecht is associate professor at the KU Leuven Institute for Healthcare Policy, Belgium. **Elly Van Bael** and **Charlotte Van der Auwera** are scientific staff at the same institute. **Deborah Seys** and **Ellen Coeckelberghs** are postdoctoral researchers at KU Leuven and **Barbara Lommers** is advisor to the general management at University Hospitals Leuven.

MANGO moment

Why are we developing a new model?

In 2001, the book *Crossing the Quality Chasm* was published in the United States. This book breaks down quality of care into six dimensions, positing that care must be safe, efficient, effective, timely, equitable and patient-centred.[1] In 2018, the World Health Organisation re-emphasised the importance of these six dimensions, but changed 'patient-centred' to 'person-centred', thereby emphasising not only the focus on preventive medicine, but also on the human being behind the patient.[2] As far as possible, caregivers should take into account the norms, values, preferences and characteristics of the individual. However, this does not mean that the patient has to be in total control. Since the beginning of this century, the main focus of caregivers, managers and policymakers has been on safe and efficient care. Now that standardisation, protocols, checklists, care pathways and evidence-based medicine have become a normal part of the care process, it is time to go back to basics and think a bit more about the person behind the patient. The focus on person-centredness has thus increased considerably over the past few years.

In this context, the KU Leuven Institute for Healthcare Policy, a research department within the Faculty of Medicine of KU Leuven in Belgium, saw it as its mission to further investigate the Mangomoment – that small gesture or unexpected mark of attention during the normal care process that takes hardly any time, resources or energy but nevertheless has a major impact. We wanted to understand whether there are any preconditions for Mangomoments and what impact they have on those involved.[3] Between November 2016 and December 2018, with the financial support of Stand Up to Cancer (www.komoptegenkanker.be), we carried out the study 'From Never to Always Events: in search of Mangomoments'.[4] This not only produced some interesting results, but also led to extra attention being paid to person-centred care.

How was the study that gave rise to the Mangomoment model carried out?

The study was initiated in three Flemish hospitals: the Imelda Hospital Bonheiden, the General Hospital Diest and University Hospitals Leuven. Patients and caregivers in oncological care departments were invited to share their experience of Mangomoments with the research team. That's how we collected the first two hundred stories. Based on these initial experiences and in close cooperation with the Stand Up to Cancer campaign team and the KU Leuven press department, we organised a media campaign to raise awareness about Mangomoments. We got coverage on the radio and television, and in newspapers and magazines. Social media brought the name, and the concept behind it, to a broader public. More than fifty healthcare organisations from Flanders and the Netherlands were willing to support the initiative. Using their internal and external communication channels, they called on all patients – not just those being treated for cancer – and their families and caregivers to share examples of Mangomoments via an automated answering service, the Mangomoment website or by putting their experiences down on paper. Anyone sharing a story could give permission for us to use it in the study or contact them for an in-depth interview. A total of 1,045 stories were shared and 351 people indicated that they were willing to be contacted for an interview. An unexpected success.

What can we learn from the 1,045 stories?

It soon became clear that what constitutes a Mangomoment is very specific. What someone enjoys is a very individual thing. It was thus no simple matter to create a ranking of the top Mangomoments that everyone would appreciate. Of the 1,045 stories, 983 (94%) could be defined as a Mangomoment. Some stories were just too big to qualify, such as organising a wedding for a palliative patient or carrying out a last major wish. Others were more negative experiences and, of course, there were also a few jokers, like the one who told us that he doesn't like mangos. We divided the 983 stories - 70% of which were sent in by patients and family members and 30% by caregivers - into seven different categories: 1) respect for values, preferences and needs; 2) emotional support; 3) involvement of family and friends; 4) physical comfort; 5) coordination of care; 6) fellow sufferers and volunteers; and 7) information, communication and education.

Of all the stories, 40% were about respect for the values, preferences and needs of the patient. That comes as no surprise. The international literature also shows that dignity and respect are priority areas for person-centred care. In addition, emotional support and attention to the involvement of family and friends were discussed in three out of ten stories. Together, these three categories account for almost 70% of the Mangomoment stories. If we focus exclusively on stories from caregivers, we see that the involvement of family and friends crops up in only 5% of the stories and that physical comfort is in third place at 13%. The top two dimensions for caregivers are respect (51%) and emotional support (18%). In oncological patients, the involvement of family and friends comes second, at 17% of the stories. For this patient group, extra attention for, and the relationship with, family and friends are therefore clear priorities. All sub-analyses show that respect for values, preferences and needs crops up most often, but that attention for family and friends is different for caregivers and patients, especially oncological patients. Caregivers, on the other hand, share more stories about offering physical comfort.

The Mangomoment model was developed by more than 800 people

In addition to the more than 1,000 stories submitted, 351 people were willing to tell the story behind their Mangomoment. The research team analysed their Mangomoments a second time and we drew up a list of people who met the criteria for an interview, ultimately inviting 67 patients, 18 family members and 35 caregivers (a total of 120 people).

The research team performed the interviews and analysed the results of the 120 interviews and these were presented to three focus groups made up of a total of 35 participants. In addition to patients, family members and caregivers, managers from healthcare organisations were also invited to attend. Finally, we summarised all the information in a single diagram, the Mangomoment model, which we presented during a final consensus meeting attended by 23 people. In addition to representatives of the groups mentioned above, policy makers and academics were also present at the consensus meeting. We made audio recordings and reports of all interviews, focus groups and the consensus meeting, and used these to provide a scientific foundation for our findings. They also provided the source material for the final scientific report on the research, which was submitted to Stand Up to Cancer.[4] Over the entire study, more than 800 people contributed information to the Mangomoment model.

After the final consensus meeting, the research team drew the definitive conclusions from the research. It's clear that Mangomoments don't just happen at random. There are preconditions and catalysts and there is the unique Mangomoment. The action or gesture has an impact on the patient and the family as well as on the caregiver in question and on the relationship between them. This Mangomoment model is explained in the figure below. We'll identify the most important parts of it.

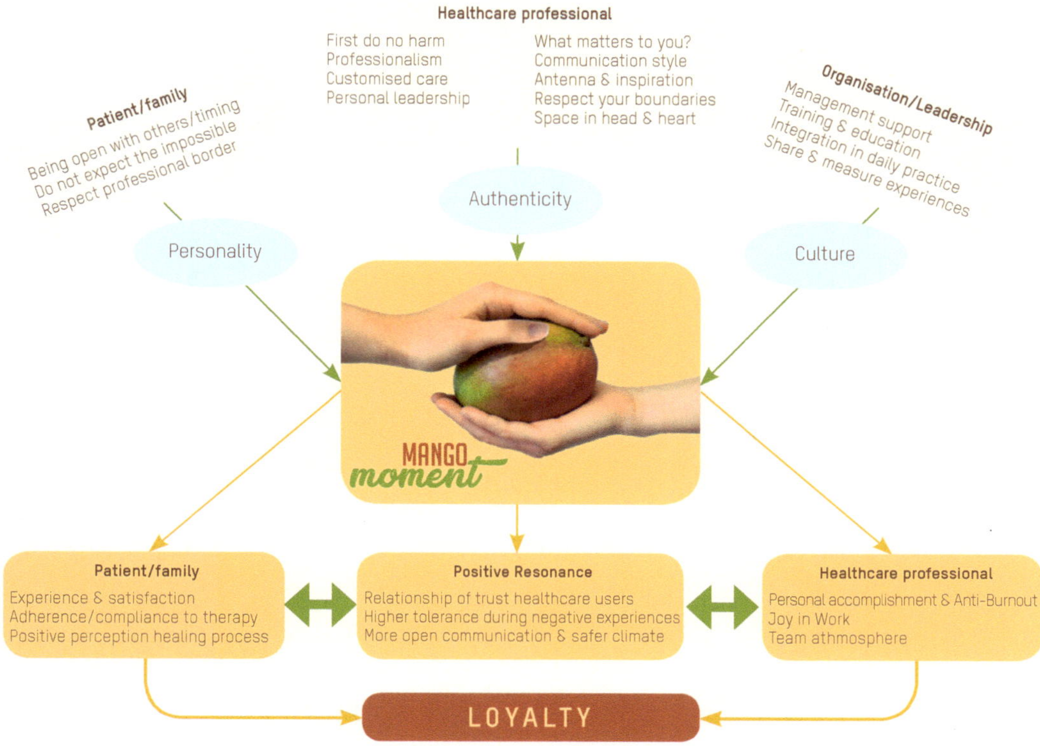

The Mangomoment model

Preconditions and catalysts

Preconditions exist not only for caregivers and healthcare organisations, but also for patients and family members, who need to be open to the action or gesture by the caregiver. And it goes without saying that timing is important and that not every gesture will be appreciated at all times. There are also boundaries that need to be respected. Firstly, there are limits to what a patient can reasonably expect and, secondly, individual caregivers will be limited by their own professional boundaries. Not all caregivers will be able to, or indeed want to, get close to the patient or family. The research also shows that the personality of the patient or family member serves as a catalyst.

Caregivers may offer Mangomoments, but must take a number of basic conditions into account. The safety of care must not be compromised. For example, a Mangomoment should never put a patient at risk of infection. Care must meet professional requirements at all times. Continuous attention should be given to personalised care. When caregivers make the effort to create a Mangomoment they often do this on the basis of personal leadership that allows them to model exemplary behaviour within the team.

In addition, there are a number of specific concerns that caregivers should bear in mind. Mangomoments are not Mangomoments if they are at odds with the value framework of the patient or family member. Knowing what is important to this unique patient is therefore of paramount importance. This makes Mangomoments a perfect match for the 'What matters to you?' movement. The caregiver needs to find out what is important to the patient, perhaps just by asking them. The caregiver cannot simply perform an action or make a gesture that is well-intentioned and that they themselves would appreciate, but that the patient may not like at all. Staff therefore need to use their communication style and sensitivity. In the study, one doctor said that you have to switch on your 'Mangomoment radar', and that this is sometimes a deliberate act. In another interview, it became clear that the radar is sometimes also deliberately switched off. In addition, examples and stories from other employees can be inspiring and there are teams that share the Mangomoment of the week with each other. Finally, caregivers will only offer that little extra if they feel good about themselves. In other words, if they have enough space in their heads and hearts to do so and if the action is compatible with their own professional boundaries. There's no point creating a Mangomoment that is not authentic, as this will not be perceived as real by the patient or their family.

In addition to preconditions for patients, family members and caregivers, there are also conditions that the organisation needs to meet. Mangomoments must be supported by the management. If the organisation's management does not attach much importance to customer-centredness, employees will not be motivated to go the extra mile. The management must set an example and support training on topics like service management. Small actions and unexpected gestures by employees need to be welcomed and facilitated. The organisation's management can support this by measuring, monitoring and communicating positive experiences. This helps to ensure that a customer-centred organisational culture is not limited to fine words during the New Year's speech by the CEO or overblown promises on the company's website and in its mission statement, but is something that is rooted into the everyday life of the organisation.

The effects of Mangomoments on patient, employee and organisation

The study shows that Mangomoments have an impact on three areas: the patient and their family, the caregiver, and the relationship that exists between them. All this makes patients, family members and caregivers more loyal to the organisation in which the Mangomoment took place. This effect indicates that Mangomoments have an impact on customer-centredness, customer loyalty and on the retention policy of an organisation.

It goes without saying that Mangomoments have a positive effect on the patient and/or their family. The interviews clearly showed that these small courtesies and gestures create a positive experience and a higher level of satisfaction. In addition to this effect, which we expected, patients also said they felt greater loyalty towards therapists with whom they have shared such an experience. Where a positive connection exists between caregivers and patients, or their family members, the caregiver's advice is more likely to be taken. Several interviews also highlighted the fact that these little things can have an important impact on the way patients feel about their healing process, with several patients saying that the small gesture suddenly gave them the energy to keep going rather than throwing in the towel.

In the interviews, caregivers as well as patients and family members talked about the positive effect a Mangomoment can have on their work and experience. Phrases like "this is what we do it for" or "this goes right to the heart of why we opted for a career in healthcare" cropped up several times. A Mangomoment can therefore trigger enthusiasm in an employee, enthusiasm that is characterised by positive energy, resilience, drive, commitment, animation, and satisfaction with both their job and the organisation itself. These characteristics tend to be lacking in employees who are prone to burnout. When Mangomoments are shared within the team and people work together to create them, this is also beneficial for teamwork, which, in turn, means that employees experience a higher level of *Joy in Work*. This concept shows how employees enjoy doing their job on a day-to-day basis. Collaboration, management support, camaraderie and being able to take on daily challenges are among the core values for greater job satisfaction and to stay healthy, happy and productive.

Perhaps the unique effect of Mangomoments is the interaction between the patient or their family and the caregiver. In her book *Love 2.0*, Professor Barbara Fredrickson from the United States calls this *positive resonance*.[5] Positive resonance is the positive chemistry and unique interaction that can arise between two individuals. Fredrickson talks about the *micromoments of positive resonance* that you need on a daily basis to feed positivism. Those little moments have a clear impact on a person's ability to function: without them, you can't take care of yourself, never mind anyone else. In a caring or customer relationship, trust develops when there is positive chemistry between the players, when they 'click'. The interviews in our study show that this positive chemistry also has an impact on tolerance. Caregivers tolerate some patients better than others. However, patients also say that, when they click with a caregiver, they find it easier to accept it when that person has a less good moment or pays them less attention due to pressure of work or even personal matters. The study also shows that, where this positive resonance exists, patients communicate more openly and honestly with the caregiver, which leads to a safer atmosphere. Patients confide in such caregivers more and feel able to express their doubts and ask any questions they have. We can thus make a link between Mangomoments and the climate of patient safety on a ward. This benefits everyone: the patient, the caregiver and the organisation.

Putting it all into practice

You can't just book a Mangomoment in on the care pathway at 10:35 am. That's not how it works. Mangomoments need to be created and can only come into being within the unique relationship between caregiver and care user. So we need to bear a number of limitations in mind and think carefully about how we can give this concept its rightful and specific place within a particular organisational structure and culture.

So, we asked a team of international experts to tell us how they see the Mangomoment concept and model. We have broken their reflections down into four sections: reflections from the patient and society, reflections from management, reflections from healthcare professionals and, finally, a number of reflections that anchor the concept within a broader context.

These reflections, together with the stories from this book and the theoretical insights from the Mangomoment model, will be used by the KU Leuven Institute for Healthcare Policy to organise training and discussion sessions in cooperation with organisations from healthcare and other industries in their joint search for warmer care , kindness and leadership.

References

1 Institute of Medicine. Committee on Quality of Health Care in America (2001). *Crossing the Quality Chasm: A New Health System for the 21st Century*. Washington: National Academies Press.

2 World Health Organization, OECD, & International Bank for Reconstruction and Development/The World Bank (2018). *Delivering Quality Health Services: A Global Imperative for Universal Health Coverage*. World Health Organization.

3 Vanhaecht, K. (2018a). In search of Mangomoments. *The Lancet Oncology, 19*(2), 165. doi:10.1016/s1470-2045(18)30034-2.

4 Vanhaecht, K. (2018b). *From Never to Always Events: op zoek naar Mangomomenten*. Consulted via https://www.komoptegenkanker.be/projecten/never-always-events-op-zoek-naar-mangomomenten.

5 Fredrickson, B.L. (2013). *Love 2.0: Finding Happiness and Health in Moments of Connection*. Hudson Street Press.

THE REFLECTION *moment* OF...

© UPC KU Leuven

It takes two to mango

Dirk De Wachter is a psychiatrist and psychotherapist. He is head of system and family therapy at the University Psychiatric Centre of KU Leuven in Kortenberg, Belgium. He works as a teacher and supervisor in family therapy in various centres at home and abroad.

It goes without saying that I wholeheartedly support the wonderful Mangomoment initiative. It is perfectly aligned with what I, like the French philosopher Emmanuel Levinas, recognise as *la petite bonté* or 'the miracle of little acts of kindness'. Levinas describes the essence of care, in which organising structures have to be overcome time and time again in a highly personal face-to-face encounter. The organisation of care systems is a necessary precondition but not in itself enough; care needs to be repeatedly rescued from dehumanisation and reduced to its essence. Within the large and complex organisations of our society, this is often what it feels like for both care users and caregivers. The well-oiled machine with its incredibly advanced technical features can achieve unprecedented performance but risks decaying into anonymity, pushing out the very essence of care in the inexorable march towards a culture of efficiency.

So, long live the mango!

But I would also like to touch upon the danger of this being endlessly recycled and hollowed out. If mangos are bought in bulk and automatically delivered to each bed along with a smiley, the gesture loses all meaning. If the Mangomoment becomes a step to be ticked off on the flow chart, with an inspection to check that it happened, it may even become counterproductive.

Mangomoments must not be hijacked by managers in a top-down policy plan to prove their superiority over the competition. Instead, managers need to leave room for non-directed bottom-up initiatives to take place spontaneously and creatively. Basically, it comes down to the cracks in the strictly targeted system, the breathing space in the busy schedule, the 'wasted' time that frees people from their functionalist pressure suits. The random act of kindness goes beyond the boundaries of the care plan to make way for a courtesy that can be almost invisible.

With or without exotic fruit, it's about the way one person sees another, the glance of recognition in a moment of humanity. A modest starting point, a small gesture that does not require any witnesses, is an important part of this. Levinas takes this concept from the novel *Zhizn i Sudba (Life and Destiny)* by Vasili Grossman, describing it as "the goodness that is condemned as stupid; an insane, harmful, blind goodness". It is clear that it is an attitude that does not really fit in with the organisational structure. It is an act of resistance, a critical corrective, an unusual event, blind, instinctive and helpless. Its greatest strength lies in this powerlessness. That's what makes it invincible; it repeatedly escapes the imminent dehumanisation that characterises all organisational structures. But paradoxically, in imperfection, in doubt, in seeking, it also supports the skeleton of the structure.

The caring, needy Other is central to the whole idea. The suffering human being, who breaks through our complacent bunker mentality and watches us uncomfortably; and the caring human being, who is capable of being powerless in humble response.

It's all about a moment of contact that lets the hope in.

To care is human

Victor M. Montori is professor of Medicine at the Mayo Clinic in Rochester, Minnesota, USA. He was born and raised in Lima, Peru. He is author and founder of *Why we revolt*, a patient revolution for careful and kind care.

Caring is a human superpower. Like self-awareness, but lovelier. Like art, but prettier. Like love, almost exactly. But this power does not need to be reminded of its great responsibility, because responding to another's need is precisely how it works.

Caring demands awareness of the needs of others and of one's ability to meet them. That superpower enables the caregiver to see beyond their own self, to notice the other, to recognize in the other their own humanity, their common humanity. As the depths of despair, illness, pain, and impotence render one person vulnerable, another one notices, witnesses, remains close, reaches out, holds, helps.

Caring is tattooed in our human DNA by the evolutionary pressure of living in community with other persons. Surviving latent under the cultural exaltation of selfishness and individualism, care knows to emerge in the hearts of complete strangers. As the footage from the disaster shows once again, these strangers, caring for and about each other, form a human chain to save that other stranger from certain death.

This superpower is also human in its contradictions. To care, the caregiver has to come closer than comfortable, stay longer than prudent, fill the air with inviting silence. Be there, restrained. Act, purposefully, effectively, generously. It is wait and see. It is both do nothing and don't just stand there. The caregiver, in caring, finds their own fears, hurts and scars exposed; their own fleshy, beating heart available to be hurt; their own battery drained by the constant effort to get the balance right: active presence and soft action. Vulnerable, giver and taker risk themselves for care to happen. While caring is exhausting and exhaustible, it is renewable, regenerating with use.

Care is a delicate superpower. Caregiving nourishes the caregiver. The inclination to care may be nurtured through love or kindled by pain. But care can also be extinguished. The caregiver may miss the other, noticing made impossible by actions that distract, by priorities that command us to shift our gaze away from the sufferer. Like ears adapting to tinnitus, caregivers can learn to ignore the persistent wailing just to simply get through the day, hearts hardened by the numbing effect of relentless pain. By exhaustion. These may lead to indifference, the opposite of care as it is also the opposite of love.

Incompetence too is the opposite of care. For care to be effective, the caregiver must invariable go beyond protocol and standards designed for the generic person to notice and respond to the one person before us. It is necessary for a clinician – any person privileged to be before the patient and care – to be present and to notice for care to happen. Yet, patients seeking healthcare often feel unseen and unheard. This is because industrial healthcare makes noticing difficult. It is hard to notice when healthcare is too fast, too crowded, too far (statistical), or too digital (where care of the patient's data is confused with care of the patient). Clinicians, even the kindest, cannot care for patients who they see as a blur, noticing nothing particular about them.

To care, one must notice, but this is not enough. The caregiver must go beyond noticing to respond effectively. Care must advance the problematic human situation of the person. What that responds must precisely entail must be uncovered in the communion between caregiver and patient. When healthcare inhibits noticing and responding, it abolishes care. It reduces the humanity of those called to care and those in need of it. This dehumanisation of patient and clinician by policies that blur patients and render clinicians ineffective at caregiving are cruel.

Clinicians cannot be expected to care as industrial healthcare cruelly adds more tasks to their to-do list, or they soon will run on empty, disappoint other patients, or disappoint themselves. Just as there is nothing between the hands in Rodin's *Cathedral*, care requires silence, room, and time to say or not, to stand and stay, to pause or act. Care opportunities demand priority, the superpower to care used wisely by leaders to delete activities not worthy of displacing care. Otherwise, care may be left to only occur by accident.

In my book, *Why We Revolt*,[1] I reflected on how amidst the cruelty of industrial healthcare, "(...) we find accidents of care. A nurse stayed after her shift to help her elderly hospital patient use his laptop to witness via live video his granddaughter's graduation. On her way home, a pharmacist took the box of medicines for a sick child traveling in Germany to the main office of the courier company after the prescription missed the last courier pickup truck. Five days after operating on his hip, the surgeon brought a chair he had at home to the patient's hotel room to make it easier for him to take a shower. Humans recognising each other as fellow humans, disappointing what others expect of them, overcoming fear and violating the care protocols to make room for care, eschewing reputation in favor of a moment of intimacy that no one had to notice."

This book is about those accidents of care. Mangomoments are demonstrations of noticing and responding, flags of the resistance against the tendency of industrial healthcare for cruelty. Yet, Mangomoments are nothing heroic, expert, or extravagant. They are signs that plain care is possible. They are small kindnesses, often perceived as extraordinary luxuries unaffordable by the pressures of high-value healthcare. They are evidence of our common vulnerabilities and fate, of our noncompliance with the ideologies and protocols of cruelty, of our standing in solidarity with each other, of our human superpower to care. They are graffiti in the experience of healthcare that calls for turning away from industrial healthcare and toward careful and kind care. They call for a patient revolution.

1 Victor Montori. *Why We Revolt: A patient revolution for careful and kind care*. The Patient Revolution, Rochester, 2017. http://patientrevolution.org/revolt

REFLECTIONS FROM PATIENT AND SOCIETY

Patient-centredness as a building block

Dave deBronkart, also known as e-Patient Dave, is a patient advocate and blogger who, in 2009, became a noted activist for healthcare transformation through participatory medicine and personal health data rights.

Ilse Weeghmans is director of the Flemish Patients' Platform.

We call for considering care and cure: For centuries we have believed that 'better care' is defined as 'better science' or 'more perfect technical skills and knowledge', but in the process, we have lost touch with the other half of healthcare: care. And ironically, it turns out that health (physical, biological health!) can be improved by caring.

Care is made up of lots of little everyday gestures: caring for our children, for our parents, for our pets, comforting one another. These are the small actions that show we care. When you are admitted into hospital as a patient, you feel at your smallest. You're afraid of what lies ahead – the pain, the uncertainty, the dreaded diagnosis, the extended period of treatment. Every patient responds to this differently because there is no such thing as *the* patient. And, as a patient, it is not just the medical side of things you worry about, but also things like how you are going to tell your children about your diagnosis or how the grandchildren are going to react when they come to visit. Like when will you get back to work? Or will you even be able to work anymore? And how are you going to manage your household in the months ahead?

Mangomoments, those very important little instants of care, are not as small as they seem because they require a caregiver to see more than just the patient and to sense what they need at that moment. And no, using the same old 'trick' won't cut it.

Dave still remembers the important kind words and small actions of a particular nurse very well: "In my worst days of 2007 when I had cancer myself, a question I sat with occasionally was 'Is the world finished with me?' At times, in the hospital, I would have a visit from a brilliant nurse practitioner, someone who has mastered both the science and the caring, as nurses must. I vividly recall one visit where, before she set about her work duties on me, she just stood at the foot of my bed and what she did was just... be with me, no words, just being with me, in the uncertainty at the cliff of existence. And in that sacred space, once, she asked peacefully: 'How are you doing?' I don't even remember what I said to her, but what I experienced was being cared for, by someone who was willing to step into that terrible uncertainty with me. It reminded me of what civil rights activist Maya Angelou said: 'But people will never forget how you made them feel.'"

"Unfortunately, you see a lot of people who once chose to care for people losing this sensitivity during or after their traineeship", says Ilse. "Pressure of work, understaffing or the structure they end up in can lead to care becoming routine, dehumanised or a purely technical matter."

In recent years, the spotlight has increasingly come to rest upon quality of life. What matters to the patient? What makes him or her happy? What brings joy? Each individual caregiver is expected to pick up on this and use it in their daily work. It will undoubtedly contribute to an increase in resilience.

Dave also experienced that the way in which you and others deal with your condition have a positive impact on the healing process. "The drug I received back then was an early immunotherapy, one that usually fails, but I was one of the lucky ones. Consider, though, that immediately at diagnosis I had chosen to use the approach of the well-known journalist and world peace advocate Norman Cousins: watching Marx Brothers movies and laughing yourself back to health. At the time nobody understood how this could be possible, but today we know more about pyscho-neuro-immunology, a newer field that finally connects (with science) our mood to our immune system. Is this what saved Cousins? We'll never know. Did it save me? All I can tell you is that my oncologist has said he wishes he could 'bottle' the way I acted, and give it to others."

Small acts of kindness in both directions between patients and caregivers are important. But this does not happen for everyone, every day and with every patient. In addition, care is no longer provided on an individual basis, but is now delivered by a team operating both inside and outside the hospital, with the patient encountering 'silos' other than those of the medical world. In this setting, small gestures make only a minimal difference: genuine patient-centred care calls for more. Patient-centred care means, first and foremost, that care is accessible and available to everyone. Thus, there needs to be broad solidarity because, without access to care, there is not even a chance of Mangomoments. Patient-centredness also means that those working in healthcare need to look beyond the medical aspects of care and take into account the person and its environment.

Can today's clinicians 'be with' a patient in a way that says 'The world is not finished with you'? Or in a way that says 'Come what may, I see you, I know you, I want to hear you. What would make you feel heard and known?' Can today's clinical experts add the further skill of somehow connecting with that being in distress, to somehow call forth the being that wants to be known and valued?

The question is how you can put these ideas into practice on a structural basis. How do you build that into the organisation of everyday care? The first step is to focus on information: working with shared files so that cooperation and coordination run smoothly. Focusing on information includes making sure the patient, too, is well informed. Studies show that well-informed patients suffer less stress and are less likely to call for assistance. Patient-centred care also means that care is coordinated across the care domains, that planning for discharge starts as soon as a patient is admitted so that cooperation and coordination with home care can be included in the plan. Patient-centred care means quality and public transparency regarding the medical side of things, but also regarding how patients feel about their care (preferably using Patient Reported Outcome Measures (PROMs) and Patient Reported Experience Measures (PREMs) developed in consultation with patients).

In addition, patients need access to their own health data, so that they can be involved in their own care. Patients are the most underused resource in healthcare and greater involvement of the patient and his environment will lead to better healthcare quality and quality of life. Therefore we need e-patients: equipped, engaged, empowered and enabled patients.

Patient-centred care involves engagement between an individual patient and their caregiver. The precondition is that the patient receives information, has access to their electronic file and is given the opportunity to participate in decisions if they so wish. Everyone agrees, but people often don't know how to put it into practice. By structural collaboration with hospitals, patient associations can provide guidance to healthcare providers. This means that patients become better informed about life with a chronic illness and are systematically referred to a patient association that can support them in the search for the renewed quality of life that awaits them. In turn, associations give feedback to the hospital about the care provided.

There are various building blocks that have to be fitted together before we can really speak of patient-centred care. Let's work on this together and let us not forget the power of small acts of kindness!

REFLECTIONS FROM PATIENT AND SOCIETY

Is gesture-based leadership what we're after?

Wilma van der Scheer holds a PhD in Health Policy and Management and is director of the Erasmus Centre for Care Management (Erasmus University Rotterdam) and chairman of the MIND Patient Platform for Mental Health.

Pauline Meurs is professor of Healthcare Management (Erasmus University Rotterdam) and chair of the Council for Public Health and Society in the Netherlands.

This book is about Mangomoments, those "small, unexpected, surprising, sometimes almost imperceptible, actions or gestures between patients, residents, family members and/or caregivers during the everyday provision of care. They take place during normal care activities, are not condition-specific and take little or no time, resources or energy." The way we see it, a Mangomoment is essentially a courtesy, a friendly gesture. Philosopher René ten Bos has studied the nature of gestures as well as *gesture-based* leadership. It is essential that the gesture is not done to achieve a particular purpose. It's not something the caregiver has to do. It is a spontaneous expression of kindness and attentiveness. The gesture must never be all about the person making it. If the gesture is sincere, it must be selfless and pure, bringing together what is beautiful and what is good. Hollow gestures are commonplace: insincere apologies, forced friendliness and smiles produced to satisfy the management. That's not what this is all about, and neither does it contribute to the goal that Kris Vanhaecht has in mind. The Mangomoment is supposed to help bring about person-centred care and customer focus.

The aim of achieving this by promoting gestures – spontaneous, disinterested acts of kindness – is a tricky undertaking and almost a contradiction in terms. There is a risk of desperation setting in, spontaneity being lost and gestures ending up being insincere and losing their value. Let's be alert to this danger. Let's embrace sincerity, warmth and spontaneity. Because, as philosopher Ten Bos teaches us, the beauty of sincere gestures is that they create communality, togetherness and connection. A Mangomoment connects patients, residents, family members and care providers in a special way. Not necessarily in a professional way, but in a human way. And professionals need that just as much as patients and their families do. From our own research in disability care, we know that having a real, warm relationship is just as important for professionals as it is for their clients, allowing them to show their best side. Patients and professionals are ordinary people who like to be seen and heard, and benefit from meaningful moments of connection and sincere gestures of kindness. It goes without saying that this is also important for family members. They want to feel that they are leaving their loved one with someone they trust, in expert and friendly hands.

One aspect of the study into Mangomoments was to "map out the most meaningful moments based upon interviews with patients, family members/ carers and healthcare professionals". The fact that patients, family members/ carers and healthcare professionals are all mentioned in the same breath is very important to us. It emphasises the reciprocity of the relationship and is a prompt to share experiences, which can open up a wealth of knowledge. Unfortunately, the experience of clients and family members has traditionally been underused in care, with the knowledge of clients and their relatives all too often not being taken seriously. The fact that patients generally know a lot about their own body, mind and life – and that it is the professional who is the layman in this regard – is often overlooked. It is time that this knowledge was put to good use.

A Mangomoment is a spontaneous gesture of kindness that can be of great value to patients and their families. As we have already mentioned, it is crucial that this is not done to achieve a particular purpose. Rather, genuinely taking client experiences seriously, studying these experiences extensively, and taking the knowledge gained in this way into account when drawing up care standards and organising care calls for systematic action, commitment and the desire to improve care, making it more personal and more valuable. We therefore conclude with the following propositions: care can be so much better if clients are seen as full-fledged partners, both in their own treatment and when carrying out research. Investigate subjects that are relevant to clients. Getting them involved in this has two benefits: the research itself will be useful and it will have a motivational effect. Every patient is also a human being with choices to make and something to contribute – particularly to their own recovery.

Mangomoments, returning kindness to health and to people

Peter Lachman is a medical doctor and the Chief Executive Officer of the Internationale Society for Quality in Healthcare (ISQUA).

"Always be a little kinder than necessary."
James M. Barrie

In 1996, my mother died following a two year battle with pancreatic cancer. I recall how she suffered with the extreme pain that characterises the disease. I was living in London, so there were many acts of kindness given to her by my friends. I recall particular Mangomoments she experienced from a friend who provided her with many small acts of kindness that allowed her to overcome the intense pain she experienced in her dying days. One was quite unique in that he purchased cannabis for her so that she could relieve the pain. I am sure this was her first experience of cannabis, and it was not available legally. Before she died, she related this small act of kindness to me and emphasised the importance of kindness in care of the ill. I did not know that this was a Mangomoment until I read the stories in this book that allowed me to reflect on the kindness she received. The stories in the book have provided the opportunity to explore the importance of kindness that define us as people who care for others.

The concept of kindness is one that has become elusive in healthcare as we have developed highly technological solutions to increasing complex situations. We are moving to the next generation of healthcare based on artificial intelligence, supported by digital health, remote medicine with wearables and sophisticated machinery. We may lose the very essence of medicine within the provision of care, namely kindness, compassion, empathy and the human touch.

With the rapid advance of medical science in the 20th century and the focus on conquering disease and ill health, medicine has possibly lost its connection with the Person as opposed to the Patient. People have become diseases to be attacked, losing their dignity in the process. Technology has replaced compassion at the centre of healthcare. This has affected both the person who receives care and the person who provides care.

The essence of healing is contained in the word kindness, which is the quality of being gentle, caring, and helpful. The people who we call patients are vulnerable in many ways. The loss of health and exposure to a new system, devoid of the usual meaning, with its own construct, means that the person becomes the patient, isolated and alone. They are separated from family, friends and familiar surroundings, and made to conform to a new paradigm. This can create an unsafe psychological environment for the person who is now a hospital number, a disease and a challenge to cure.

A person who becomes a patient often gives up their rights as a person. The system that is designed to treat disease turns the person into a number to be processed, rather than viewing the patient as a person who is afraid, apprehensive, confused, without control, but who also has a family and a life outside of the illness. The hospital as a concept is not designed for people to receive care but rather for people to deliver care.

A by-product of the design of healthcare is the increasing alienation of people delivering care as the way we have designed healthcare services can result in lack of meaning and belonging for clinical staff. Increased use of technological interventions, computerisation, digitalisation and complex working conditions have led to the isolation of healthcare providers from the core value of compassion and empathy. This is evidenced in the increased reporting of burnout and distress in healthcare providers.

In response to this alienation felt by people receiving care, we have introduced the concept of person-centred care, which is a reaction to the dominant technological approach to healthcare. The concept of person-centred care concentrates on health as opposed to healthcare or disease management. However, for person-centred care to be successful in the high-tech construct of a hospital it has to overcome major barriers as the environment has not been designed to deliver care designed by people for people. Rather healthcare delivery has been designed by healthcare professionals for patients. People often have not been given the opportunity to co-design the way they wish to be treated. The current design of care seems to have taken away the humanity that makes a patient a person.

Person-centredness asks how we can achieve health in both body and mind. This can be attained by focussing on the spiritual nature of healing that is the foundation of caring, the touching of the inner being of the person rather than mainly focussing on the treatment of the ailment or disease. Once that is the goal of care, then the management of the symptoms of disease can be so much more easily reached. Person-centredness is all embracing and the core of this is the values of compassion with kindness, respect, partnership and holistic care. At the centre of true person-centred care is the concept of compassion and kindness which accepts the individual as a whole, body and mind being inseparable. Being kind helps one to ensure there is respectful interactions where the inner feelings are as important as the external demeanour. The domains of quality were originally introduced by the Institute of Medicine (IOM) in *Crossing the Quality Chasm,* published in 2001, as safe, effective, efficient, timely, equity and patient-centred. These dimensions then play supporting roles in attaining the goal of health. From 2018 onwards IOM and other authors include also accessibility in the dimension timely and the dimension patient-centred changed into person-centred.

The six domains are technical, and one has to add the current challenge of climate chance by being kind to the environment (eco-friendly). We need to move from the purely technical to the true values of health empathy and kindness with these values of dignity, respect, partnership and compassion at the core for both people who receive care and for those who provide care. This will transform the domains of quality from a technical unfeeling approach to one that has people in the middle. If we add kindness to the recipe of quality then we move back to the vision of the healer of the mind and soul, as well of the body.

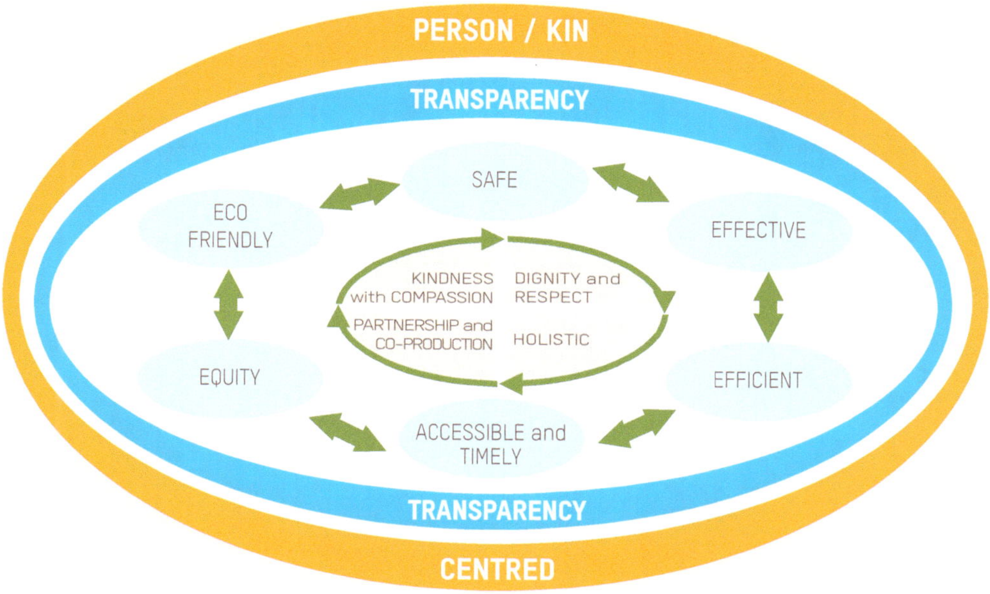

The uniqueness of a Mangomoment is its ability to be an expression of kindness not only to the person as a patient but also to the healer as a person. This moment of kindness that takes no effort other than a brief moment of giving, returns the Professional to be a Person, and as a result the Patient becomes a Person as well. This intervention addresses the alienation felt by both patients and their carers in hospital. A Mangomoment is an expression of kindness, an act that has mutual benefit for the psychological safety of patients and clinical staff.

I have been fortunate to travel widely to different cultural contexts. In South Africa the concept of 'Ubuntu' or "the belief in a universal bond of sharing that connects all humanity" is the equivalent of the concept of the Mangomoment. Ubuntu incorporates the essence of humanity that is shown in the Mangomoment.

As I consider the growing understanding of the need to develop psychological safety for both the person as provider and person as patient, the stories of Mangomoments have built a reservoir of goodwill and peace between healer and healed. It is a way to build resilience and healing, kindness and understanding and cannot be dismissed as an insignificant event.

The future of healing will be strengthened and be more secure if we collect these stories and use them to help us overcome the challenges that we face in the complexity of facilitating health and improving healthcare.

Mangos grow where the climate is right

Herman Daems is chairman of KU Leuven and emeritus professor. He has built up an impressive track record, both academically and in the business world, and has taught at numerous foreign universities and business schools, including Harvard.

Mangos don't grow just anywhere. They are found only in tropical and subtropical areas, where the climate is right for them. I believe the same applies to Mangomoments. Whereas mangos depend upon the climate to flower and grow, Mangomoments depend on the organisational climate. A Mangomoment is the little gesture by a caregiver or service provider who wants to pamper a patient or customer for once or give someone a bit of individual attention. In some organisations, Mangomoments are common, in others they are a bit of a rarity. Just as mangos need a particular climate to flower and grow, Mangomoments also seem to need a certain organisational climate if they are to flourish. So, what conditions need to be in place within an organisation for Mangomoments to thrive?

I am convinced that if we want to create more Mangomoments within an organisation, we should start not at the bottom of the organisation, but right at the top. It's a commonly held belief that all you need to do to create more Mangomoments is to make staff aware of their importance. I don't think that's true. First and foremost, we need to ensure that bosses create Mangomoments for their staff. Organisations where staff are attentive to their patients and clients are the ones in which bosses care about their staff, and show it. Organisations where caregivers and service providers snarl at patients and customers, are the ones where bosses snarl at employees. I know of hardly any examples where it is the other way around.

I haven't researched this theory scientifically and I don't know if that's ever been done. I assume it has, but after years of observation of organisations, I am convinced that it is correct. Customer-friendly, patient-driven organisations have employee-friendly bosses. Staff adopt the behaviour of their supervisors. What employees experience in their working environment is passed on to patients and customers. Why does that happen? I believe there are four reasons, all of which relate to the way that organisations are structured and function. This means that we can intervene in that structure and its functioning and hopefully stimulate Mangomoments within an organisation.

The first reason is that employees behave in the way they think bosses and managers want and expect them to behave. They think that, by copying the boss's behaviour, they will get on their manager's good side and improve their chances when it comes to their annual performance review.

The second reason relates to the duties assigned to the employee by their manager or those higher up in the organisation. If their duties include too many administrative tasks and leave little time and space for Mangomoments, this will give the employee the message that Mangomoments are not all that important to the management. This conclusion will be reinforced if the management makes the correct performance of administrative tasks central to the employee's performance review and perhaps even a condition for receiving a bonus.

The third reason is that many organisations look at things from the inside out, focussing on their to-do list and on how efficiently tasks are performed. Few look at things from the outside in, meaning that they don't know enough about the way patients or customers perceive the organisation. As a result, ideas for Mangomoments don't emerge spontaneously. There is a feeling that if the organisation is functioning properly it is doing well, even though this is nothing to do with how patients and customers perceive the organisation.

The previous reasons were negative; they are all about why creating Mangomoments is difficult. But there is also a positive side to things. If managers talk about Mangomoments in a positive way and create Mangomoments themselves, the number of Mangomoments can increase rapidly.

In a highly digitised world in which care and service provision are becoming increasingly automated and robotised and in which not only self-service but also self-care is now becoming a reality, Mangomoments are crucial if we are to keep the focus on human beings. But the number of Mangomoments that take place depends on the extent to which the management and organisation of the institution providing the care or services are prepared to incorporate Mangomoments into the structures and functioning of the organisation. Mangos, like apples, never fall far from the tree. If the management and organisation contribute positively, Mangomoments will grow. This will benefit patients and customers, but it will also mean that caregivers and service providers will gain more pleasure from their work.

REFLECTIONS FROM MANAGEMENT

The hospital as a hospice in the era of GDPR

Mark Waer is chairman of the executive committee of University Hospitals Leuven and full professor at KU Leuven.

Wim Robberecht is managing director of University Hospitals Leuven and full professor at KU Leuven.

Doctors don't like the phrase 'customer-centred': it has connotations of commercialism, setting it at odds with the relationship of trust between doctor and patient. Rather than talking about customer-centred care, we prefer to talk about patient-centred care, which goes above and beyond customer focus. A patient wants to be seen not as a research object or case, not as a client or customer, and not as a cardiac or cancer patient, but as a whole person, as a human being. In the era of the General Data Protection Regulation (GDPR), digitisation and patient empowerment this holistic attitude can prove a challenge.

The emancipation of the patient is without doubt a positive and irreversible trend. Patients are becoming more assertive and better informed, and they expect a lot from healthcare institutions. They organise themselves in patient associations, gain access to their patient files, and are equal partners in decisions about the healing process or their end of life care. Thanks to Belgian law on patients' rights, patients are seen as 'customers' who are entitled to healthcare, clear information and privacy. The 2002 Act formally established the link between caregiver and patient, whilst at the same time improving the quality of medical care.

No one wants to see us go back to the paternalistic relationship between doctor and patient. The idea of the doctor as someone who knows best and makes all the decisions no longer fits into our new society. But there is another, less negative and more fatherly, aspect to this paternalism: the doctor who is concerned, the caregiver who picks up on this. Patients who unite in organisations are in a stronger position, but there is a danger that this will lead to a society that is concerned only with the average and the majority, and disregards the exception or those in a minority. Computerisation provides greater safety and clarity, but we need to avoid requirements such as informed consent and transparency in patient records resulting in caregivers adopting a defensive attitude, patients having to provide their signature as if signing a contract, and insurance companies wanting to insure against every single risk. Personal relationships, and the relationship between doctor and patient in particular, cannot be set down in a contract. The tendency to codify our sky-high expectations regarding customer-centred care in laws and procedures is understandable, but a doctor-patient relationship can and should transcend this.

The Mangomoment has come at the right time in this trend. It reminds us that there can be room for warmth, affection and empathy that goes beyond mere medical interaction or customer-centred kindness. How can we, as the hospital management, encourage holistic patient-centred care? Everyone knows what a high workload doctors, nurses and other healthcare professionals have. Capacity problems, increases in administrative workload, accreditations, quality and safety procedures or interdisciplinary consultations mean there is often too little time even for the necessary medical care. And, in teaching hospitals, doctors have to fulfil a role as researchers and teachers as well as carrying out their caring duties.

But it is precisely this link with the university that inspires us to continue seeing ourselves as a hospice rather than a hospital, an idea that is echoed in the name of the Gasthuisberg campus (*gasthuis* being a hospice). KU Leuven has a long-standing tradition of personalism, a philosophy that sees a human being not only as an individual, but also as a person who exists through and for interpersonal relationships. Even in a hospital full of specialists, it is possible to remain open to that personal relationship between patient and caregiver. It doesn't need to take much time. There is no checklist, procedure or time limit for a holistic, more empathetic approach – it is more a question of the right attitude. It can be enough just to listen to a patient's story or to let them know that you have heard them as a human being, rather than just as a patient. A hospital can radiate customer-centredness down to the smallest details, such as a warm welcome at reception, the helpfulness of the cleaning staff during a stay in hospital or the attentiveness of the doctor on discharge day.

What can hospital policy do to encourage this human and personal approach to a patient? The human resources department can bear it in mind when recruiting medical staff by not only choosing the most brilliant medical profiles but also considering the human qualities of doctors and nurses. And the hospital management can ensure that its employees are made aware of the hospital's mission and values, which includes shelving ideas that conflict with this patient-centred approach.

In addition, as befits good scientists, we can live by the principle 'to measure is to know' by conducting patient surveys and staying alert to patient feedback. Last but not least, as hospital management, we can also set a good example by letting people know how important these values really are to us. For example, by creating Mangomoments for employees and treating them with the same holistic values of respect, empathy and warm affection that we expect them to show in their dealings with patients. Because if we are to be a customer-centred organisation, hospital staff also need to respect each other and feel that the hospital policy is on their side. Another thing we can do is to keep on asking ourselves 'have we given someone a Mangomoment today?'

Robots and Mangomoments: can they co-exist?

Margot Cloet is managing director at Zorgnet Icuro, the association of Flemish hospitals and nursing homes, Belgium.

Fenna Heyning is director at the association of specialised hospitals (STZ), the Netherlands.

Few will disagree that innovation and care go hand in hand. Just think of the importance of the invention of soap and the discovery of water purification systems for our healthcare. These may not be the first things that spring to mind when we talk about innovation, but there are still parts of the world where these represent a tremendous breakthrough and can bring about major health gains. In other regions, concepts such as artificial intelligence, health apps, information storage via wearables, robotics, exoskeletons or medtech have become indispensable in the healthcare sector. Those so-called emerging health technologies are used in many types of disease prevention and treatment. They have taken such an important place in healthcare that they have radically changed the nature of the healthcare relationship, and will continue to do so. Some even claim that technology is set to replace everything that human beings currently do. Take robotics in elderly care for example. What's the relationship between technology and care in this setting? Do we want robots to gradually replace human care workers (nurses, paramedics, healthcare professionals, etc.)? Or should robots be playing a supporting role? In fact, the answer to these questions is related to another question: should we introduce robots in elderly care to compensate for the shortage of care staff, or do we see robots first and foremost as a means of improving the quality of care?

We firmly believe that innovative techniques go hand in hand with care provided by human beings; that the two are complementary and can even enhance one another. For example, technological innovation in healthcare can free up time for high-quality human care. What are we to make of the fact that some patients or residents prefer to be washed by a robot rather than by a human caregiver, seeing the robot as a full-fledged replacement for the nurse or carer? Could it be that this choice is rooted in their experience of poor human care? It is perhaps no great surprise that patients or residents prefer to be washed by an ever-friendly and endlessly patient robot rather than by a surly nurse in an enormous hurry who makes them feel like they are a difficult obstacle getting in the way of a tight care schedule. This example makes it clear to us that technological innovation in healthcare must support, rather than push out human care so that it can enhance the quality of healthcare in the interests of all citizens, not least the healthcare workers themselves.

We use two different standards to judge technology and care: technology needs to be efficient, whilst care needs to be humane. These two assessment criteria mean that we should always maintain a critical stance when considering the integration of technological innovation into a healthcare setting. There is a real danger of the efficiency criterion taking precedence over human dignity.

So, what does this have to tell us about Mangomoments? First and foremost, that even in times of technological innovation in healthcare, the relational aspect must always be part of good healthcare because good healthcare is, by definition, relational. The quality of care after all stands or falls by the quality of the care relationship and this book teaches us that Mangomoments always come into being in the context of a human care relationship. Returning to our example of robotics: robots alone cannot create Mangomoments, but they can create the context in which it is easier for human caregivers to allow their patients or residents to experience Mangomoments.

Mangomoments will not solve public health problems

Massimiliano Panella is the Director of the School of Public Health at UPO University in Novara, Italy. He is also the Director of the MPH program in Lifestyle Medicine and the President of the European Pathways Association. Next to his academic activity, he was Chief Medical Officer of the Saint Andrew Hospital in Vercelli and of the Department of Primary Care at the Health Authority in Vercelli, Italy.

In 1920, Charles-Edward Amory Winslow defined Public Health as "the science and art of preventing disease, prolonging life and promoting human health through organized efforts and informed choices of society, organizations, public and private, communities and individuals".

My friend and colleague Kris Vanhaecht introduced and defined in 2018 the Mangomoment concept as "small unexpected acts or gestures, which are of great value in the care experience of patients, residents, families and healthcare professionals. They take place during normal care activities and ask nearly no additional resources, time or energy."

During our talks, Kris and I reflected a lot on the possible impact of Mangomoments from a public health perspective. We both considered a Mangomoment as a person-centred public health intervention that should be implemented in healthcare systems. Moreover, it can be considered as a health promotion intervention because of its positive effect on health (including positivism in life, motivation, etc.). In other words, here arose the question that I will answer in this small contribution: Can Mangomoments be considered a public health intervention and consequently be recommended and implemented at this level?

If we look at Winslow's definition, that has characterized the last 100 years of the history of public health, the answer is quite easy, and it is "probably not ...". But this discipline has early roots in antiquity and is moving fast into the future. So, let's take a travel machine and see if we can change our perspective.

The first stop of our time machine is Ancient Greece. In Greek as well as Roman mythology, Hygieia was one of the Asclepiadae; the sons and daughters of the god of medicine, Asclepius. Asclepius was associated with healing, while Hygieia - as the goddess and personification of health, cleanliness and hygiene more directly associated with healing - was associated with the prevention of sickness and the continuation of good health. Hygieia was imported by the Romans as Valetudo, the goddess of personal health, but after a while, she was increasingly identified with the ancient Italian goddess of social welfare, Salus. Therefore, a special thanks to Dr. Winslow for his definition, but no doubts left: Hygieia is the first public health 'doctor'!

The question is now: how can this ancestor of the modern public health professionals be related to Mangomoments? Hygieia, "gracious goddess whose noble heart and healing hands are well known to all, kindly giver of strength and hearty good health to mankind" healed the patients by helping them "to find their own way to wellness and wholeness" and "to become the ones who seeks the good". At that time, people defined this special relation between a doctor and his patient as a moment of pray. Today, thanks to Viviane and Annemie Struyf, we can define it as a Mangomoment.

Now let's go back to the present. In the 21st century the way public health aims to solve problems has significantly improved compared to 1920 (i.e. the time of Winslow), and this particularly thanks to the public health 2.0 initiative. Public health 2.0 is a movement within public health that aims to make public health activities more accessible to the general public and more user driven. Public health 2.0 draws on ideas from web 2.0 like crowdsourcing and spontaneous knowledge sharing, and aspires to apply these processes to make health promotion and prevention more understandable, feasible and, therefore, accessible. In my opinion, the collection and sharing of information about Mangomoments could represent a good example of a public health 2.0 initiative, because of its positive effect on improving the quality of healthcare activities making them more understandable and, why not, more human and friendly for the public.

Public health is moving quickly into the future, and information sharing, and user centred design of care is just one of its current and future challenges. To address worldwide key health issues, the United Nations have developed the Sustainable Development Goals building off the Millennium Development Goals of 2000 which are set to be completed by 2030. These goals are mainly focused on fighting health disparities. The health issues related to poverty, hunger and food security, health, education, gender equality and women's empowerment, and water and sanitation, probably will not be solved by Mangomoments, but I am sure that also in the future every new Mangomoment will help us to make public health a little sweeter.

The Mangomoment is the icing on the cake, but let's not forget the cake itself

Wim Schellekens is a former general practitioner, hospital administrator and chief inspector of the healthcare inspectorate, the Netherlands.

Dirk Ramaekers is a general internist, medical director of the Jessa Hospital and part-time professor at the KU Leuven Institute for Healthcare Policy.

In Mangomoments we've rediscovered how important ordinary, everyday things can be to patients. In an evidence-based, industrialised healthcare system, Mangomoments show our blind spot, where caregivers sometimes fail in paying sufficient attention to those little moments that are important to patients. Obviously people don't go to their doctor or into hospitals to experience a Mangomoment; they want the best possible care in an acceptable timeframe, and receive good and understandable information about their condition. The Mangomoment should be something extra – the icing on the cake.

But what about the cake itself? Since we have been measuring the quality of care, we have seen a large and mostly hard to explain variation between different doctors and hospitals. There's a major variety in risk of infection after surgery between hospitals. For some cancers, the probability of survival when being treated at high expertise centres is twice as high compared to centres with little experience. In one nursing home, medication safety is a top priority, whilst in others you will find polypharmacy and errors. On average, our care may score very well compared to international numbers, but our current system has not succeeded in reducing this inexplicable variation sufficiently. This is bad news, as it means that patients are not necessarily receiving good care everywhere, which undermines confidence in the healthcare system. And, of course, the best icing in the world won't make up for an inedible cake. This is why professionals and policymakers need to focus primarily on 'the cake', i.e. on the question of how we make healthcare increasingly effective, safe, timely and patient-centred. It goes without saying, doesn't it?

In the year 2020, patients take it for granted that the care they receive is safe: that they will be given the right medication on the right time and in the correct dosage, that doctors and nurses will wash their hands and communicate effectively so that misunderstandings are ruled out, that anticoagulation will be stopped at the right time during surgery, that their general practitioner will be properly informed when they are discharged from the hospital, and so on. If those things don't happen, there is a high probability of harm. And if everything does run smoothly, the patient rightfully perceives it as something normal. What kind of patient would leave a hospital and starts raving about how good it was because he didn't get an infection, because he wasn't being mixed up with another patient or because there weren't any compresses and wadding left behind inside him after surgery?

We know by now that patient safety is by no means a self-evident something. Working even more intensively on patient safety and investing more in watertight systems to prevent these risks remains a major responsibility for healthcare professionals and hospital administrators alike. After all, what's the use of a Mangomoment if the patient has suffered serious and avoidable damage?

We would like to finish by saying a few words about measuring quality. In the Netherlands, and more recently also in Flanders, patients have an increasingly accessibility to quality indicators. But these always show a small part of the cake. A plethora of – sometimes difficult to understand – figures can make it difficult to get an overview of what's really going on.

Why don't we ask patients more often how they have experienced their care, and what could be improved? This could be done in several ways. Patient experience can be measured using surveys or so-called Patient Reported Experience Measures, and patients can also be directed personally. For example, some hospital staff interview patients every month, asking questions such as 'What do you like about this hospital?' or 'If you were in charge, what would you change?' Some hospitals have a 'host' at the emergency department or on the ward. There is even a hospital that introduced the first-ever patient experience officer. All these initiatives show that we are looking for ways to improve the patient experience. There is a growing awareness of the fact that hospitals must put their patients at the centre of care, and that production, machines and personnel are simply tools to provide high-quality care.

A patient can easily tell if he has received special attention under the form of a Mangomoment, but there are other important aspects of quality that they find hard or impossible to assess. The test or treatment may have been carried out carefully in terms of quality, but was it even necessary in the first place? Overconsumption and overly profit-oriented care can be detrimental to quality of care and patient safety. Professionals need to measure this in a more targeted way and hold each other to account. Not to check up on each other, or for the management or the inspection, but simply due to it being inherent to professionalism.

Measuring indicators is meaningful, educational and often enjoyable. Accountability for improvements is not a crime. Constant measuring, learning and improving makes to an ever better cake. Only then Mangomoments can take their rightful place as the delicious icing.

Mangomoments in a time of nursing shortages

Hester Vermeulen is affiliated to the IQ Scientific Center for Quality of Healthcare of the Radboud University Medical Centre and to the HAN University of Applied Sciences.

Walter Sermeus is full professor at the KU Leuven Institute for Healthcare Policy. He led the RN4Cast collaborative and is the leader of the Magnet4Europe consortium.

The healthcare system is under a lot of pressure. On the one hand, budgets are tight. On the other, the system is facing increasing demand due to the ageing population and increased levels of multimorbidity. And caregivers themselves are getting older as well. A shortage of 400,000 physicians and 2.5 million nurses is expected by 2030 within the 32 countries of the Organisation for Economic Cooperation and Development (OECD). The World Health Organisation, together with the United Nations, has made the fight against these shortages a priority.

This leads to very high workload for nurses. The RN4CAST study, based upon research in twelve European countries in which more than 30,000 nurses and 11,000 patients were surveyed, mapped out nurse numbers and linked these to quality of care and job satisfaction amongst nurses. Results showed a 7% increase in the number of deaths for each additional patient a nurse has to care for. One important explanation for the higher mortality rate is that nurses do not have time to perform essential care, such as surveillance on patients after surgery. This means it takes longer to assess potential complications, increasing the risk of death. In hospitals where nurses report better working conditions, patients are more satisfied with their care. Not surprisingly, working conditions can also be linked to the wellbeing of nurses, measured by factors such as burnout and intent to leave. This is a concern for many boards. Shortages on the labour market and in the budget often lead to less-than-ideal numbers of nurses, resulting in lower quality, dissatisfaction among patients and staff, and higher staff turnover. This in turn increases workload and makes the institution less attractive to work in. How do we get out of that vicious circle?

Mangomoments may offer an escape route. These moments don't take much time, but a small gesture can be exactly what is needed to show nurses and patients alike that they are appreciated as human beings. Although Mangomoments usually feel spontaneous, they often come down to good leadership as this is what creates a positive and innovative working environment with room for person-centred care.

"I saw the tears in my husband's eyes. He went along to an exhibition at the Day of Nursing, where photographs of special moments of care were displayed. One of the photographs showed an intensive care patient whose burning last wish – to see his dog again – was granted. 'That's nice, isn't it?' he said, 'That's nursing leadership.'

Leadership is different from management. Leadership is all about innovation, influence and inspiration and is focussed primarily on people, whereas management is often about administration and monitoring and is focussed mainly on processes. Nursing leadership has been a hot topic in the Netherlands and Belgium over the past two years, and this has been backed up by action as well as words. Carers, nurses and nursing specialists have turned into genuine rebels lately, drawing attention to the enormous administrative burden and also coming up with solutions to save time. Time that can be spent on essential care that is frequently left undone at the end of a shift. The solutions revolve around important tasks such as patient education, which gives patients and their families back control over their own illnesses and lives, and also comforting patients and providing a listening ear.

This person-centredness allows Mangomoments to flourish. It sometimes takes courage, as shown by the example of the dog in intensive care: courage to bend the rules, courage to enter into debate and courage to genuinely think in terms of quality of life and how to achieve it. It can also be about small things, like making sure that a 90-year-old woman can eat rabbit with stewed pears again on Christmas Eve – something she kept telling me her mother used to make. Taking time and space to really listen to people's stories and then adapting individual care based on what you have heard not only keeps patients and their families happy, but also keep staff happy and increases job satisfaction amongst nurses. Moreover, it offers a way out of the negative spiral described above.

REFLECTIONS FROM HEALTHCARE PROFESSIONALS

The zest of the mango

Anne Vandenhoeck is an assistant professor at the Faculty of Theology and Religious Studies at KU Leuven and chair of the Academic Centre for Practical Theology. She is also director of the European Research Institute for Chaplains in HealthCare (ERICH).

Simon Evers is a spiritual caregiver at the OLVG hospital in Amsterdam. He was chairman of the Association for Spiritual Care Professionals in the Netherlands and is the current coordinator of the European Network for HealthCare Chaplains (ENHCC).

Mangomoments add zest to care in two senses. On the one hand, they are what care is all about – the zest of the mango, if you will. It's a question of realising you have a real human being in front of you, of seeing the whole person. Not the liver in room three, but Mrs. x with liver disease in room three. Seeing the person behind the patient calls for a relationship-based vision and a clear perspective on what good care is. Thus, Mangomoments show us what care is really about. But they do more than that: they also add zest to healthcare. Zesty care is shot through with Mangomoments that build resilience. This way, Mangomoments are a symptom of compassionate or warm care.

Concern for what profoundly moves people, what motivates and supports them, and what gives them resilience, goes to the heart of our job as spiritual caregivers. In studies, patients say that they particularly value being able to talk to spiritual caregivers about their thoughts and feelings. If patients appreciate this, it is because these caregivers really try to listen to the patient and make time for them. These conversations often revolve around the meaning that patients find (or fail to find) in their relationship with their body, with others, with society, with nature or with whatever is meaningful or sacred to them. Mangomoments arise naturally from the knowledge of what sustains, invigorates and gives resilience to the patient at the deepest level. The patient is the greatest source of inspiration for this.

In a conversation with a spiritual caregiver, a 91-year-old woman revealed that she was still grieving for a premature baby she had lost. She had never seen her child and didn't know what had become of it. The spiritual caregiver recognised this as an obstacle in the life balance that the elderly woman was drawing up and decided to try and find out more. Working with a gynaecologist, the administrative services and the hospital archives, he was able to find out the reason for the death and where her baby was buried. At his request, the head of the cemetery produced a burial certificate and the gynaecologist wrote a thoughtful letter explaining the death. This was invaluable to the patient, who was finally able to come to terms with the loss of her baby and overcome her feeling of unrest about its fate. When she returned home, she wrote a touching thank-you card to the spiritual caregiver.

Compassionate care begets compassionate care. It can be as simple as that. One caregiver sees another providing warm care and is inspired to do the same. This creates a culture that is beneficial to everyone, including the caregivers themselves. It's not just a question of the good feeling you get when you do something nice for a patient, it's also about being open to a degree of reciprocity. What it boils down to is allowing people to take care of you, too. Care is a deeply relational thing and not always a one-way street. One simple manifestation is when a patient waits before asking to be sat upright because they can see the nurse is particularly busy at that moment.

But sometimes patients also create genuine Mangomoments for caregivers. Steven had been in hospital waiting for a heart transplant for a long time and was connected to an external heart pump. He had a good relationship with his spiritual caregiver: she got his sense of humour and he appreciated her faithful visits. They talked about Steven's upbringing, the values that were important to him, his belief in 'something' and his voluntary work for the fire brigade. When the spiritual caregiver left to work in another hospital, her colleagues held a farewell party. Steven appeared with a bowl of homemade fruit salad, which he had taken great pains to prepare himself in the ward's kitchen. This gesture meant a lot to both the spiritual caregiver and to Steven himself.

For spiritual caregivers, Mangomoments are spontaneous acts of committed, warm care that happen in the relationship with the patient and their loved ones and are based on their spiritual needs and resources. They can also be a sign of gratitude or appreciation from patients to caregivers. These moments are most likely to occur, and have the best chance of success, in a compassinate, warm-hearted culture of care.

About triangles and the importance of happy doctors

Herwig Van Dijck is a pathologist at the Sint-Maarten General Hospital Mechelen (Belgium), a staff member at KU Leuven and has a leading role in the Flemish association of Chief Medical Officers.

Sander de Hosson is a lung specialist with specific interest in palliative care at the Wilhelmina Hospital in Assen, a blogger and columnist in the Netherlands.

In 2018, 'Mangomoment' almost became the word of the year in Flanders and the Netherlands. The phrase represents an important development in healthcare, calling upon us to be more than simply healthcare technicians but to fulfil our role as doctors with compassion and empathy. It is a real-world manifestation of the finding that contented patients heal better and happy caregivers provide better care, and is along the same lines as the related movement in the industrial world. Happy employees are better employees.

Is our sector lagging behind in this area? Perhaps not, but insufficient attention has been paid to the extraordinary importance of compassion. The Mangomoment initiative, and others like it, demonstrate that our vision of what constitutes good care is gradually changing. As we move forward, we will have to give more thought to the question of how we are to embed compassion into a systematic, structural approach. This is not mere hype, but a crucial change to the way we think about medicine. We can't go back to the old ways of doing things; rather, we need to capitalise on this momentum and follow the course that has been set. Because of the pressure that most caregivers are under, that will be quite a challenge.

Mangomoments come into being within the triangle made up of the patient or client, the environment and the care team. Doctors have always been important partners within this care team and take on a great deal of responsibility. Mangomoments are only possible if each side of the triangle is sufficiently well supported – in other words, if it is strong enough – to spontaneously trigger Mangomoments. We are therefore against the introduction of any additional committees or metrics. We need to ensure that there are sufficient supports in place within the healthcare team and its environment to produce moments of visible value for the patient or client, spontaneously and informally, as part of the continuum of everyday care.

So, how do we do that? This is no easy task, but it is in line with the initiatives to prevent burnout among caregivers and help them deal with stress and emotional pressure that are becoming increasingly popular. It boils down to paying attention to the human being behind the caregiver and to their own personal perspective and experience.

It is very important that this should start in the early stages of any training course. This interpretation of the caregiver's role is an intrinsic part of their duties and not something that can be tacked on as an afterthought. We know that there are already initiatives in this area, and that these are set to grow and will, by trial and error, become a permanent feature of training programmes. Investing in self-care for the caregiver, and for the team as a whole, has the potential to create unprecedented added value that will bear fruit in the form of Mangomoments. We need to be creating these not only for our patients and clients, but also for every caregiver and staff member within the care process.

Doctors and managers in the healthcare sector therefore have a twofold role. First and foremost, they need to develop a good personnel policy for care teams and other employees in the care institution. They can also support the process by valuing, and complimenting, any Mangomoments that arise. If not enough of these Mangomoments take place they may ask themselves whether 'something is going wrong in human resources policy'. Mangomoments are an indicator of strong, healthy care teams and institutions, and their absence a worrying indicator of the need to tackle these issues at grassroots level.

Medical technical services such as laboratories or pathological anatomy, as well as services where patients are present only briefly, such as the x-ray department, should not isolate themselves from this whole movement. Part of the strength of clinical services lies in its effective, fast and accurate support for all the aspects cited above. Engaging proactively in the care process, and making it all just that little bit easier, can make a world of difference.

Finally, a word about environmental factors. When new care institutions are built, a lot of attention is paid – and quite rightly so – to the caregiver's workplace and the patient environment. But minor adjustments to that environment can facilitate major steps forward in the field of compassion. Little things like subdued lighting, greater use of colour, and art on the wall, are easily overlooked details that can give us more leverage to create Mangomoments for the caregiver, the healthcare institution and, last but not least, for the person that it's all about: our patient or client.

The virtue of the Mangomoment

Yvonne Denier is an associate professor in health ethics at KU Leuven and senior advisor at Zorgnet Icuro, Belgium.

Paul van Tongeren is emeritus professor of philosophical ethics at Radboud University Nijmegen and KU Leuven.

For many, the subject of ethics in healthcare conjures images of ethical committees and working groups discussing difficult dilemmas based on a range of ethical theories and value frameworks. By a process of reflection, dialogue and consultation (moral deliberation) a satisfactory outcome is sought for a pressing situation or tricky dilemma.

In such cases, it helps if those within the healthcare organisations in question have a mission or vision that highlights the core values that guide the organisation and expresses its ethical identity. This identity is often further detailed in advisory texts, policy documents or discussion papers that set down the ethical vision for particular areas and subareas of care (such as end-of-life care, restriction of freedom, early care planning, etc.). It is also addressed by specific codes and protocols in which the ethical principles of the healthcare organisation are translated into specific standards, guidelines and codes of practice (for example on euthanasia or artificial feeding and fluid delivery). But abstract values and compelling standards must be rooted in virtues: well-formed attitudes that allow people to home in on those values so that they are able to do the right thing in specific situations almost without thinking.

In the context of values and standards, ethics is often associated with expert committees and serious individuals who act as 'ethical experts' to translate existing scientific theories into real-world practice. In one way or another, we want to get to grips with the ethical questions and dilemmas in healthcare so that we can provide a well-founded answer within an integrated organisational and ethical structure. But we must not forget the other component of ethics in healthcare, namely the perspectives and fundamental attitudes from which the specific care relationship between care providers, care users and their relatives springs when one person meets the other in a spirit of attentiveness.

Testimonies about Mangomoments teach us that it is precisely the small, almost invisible but nevertheless very real, actions that are so important to patients. Little moments of unexpected enjoyment brought about by a listening ear or tiny gesture, a 'normal conversation' about cows and calves instead of constant immersion in medical jargon, a reassuring word before going into surgery, a hand on the shoulder, a compliment, a hair wash, a film afternoon especially for you in your hospital room – or by eating a mango. These are the moments of real connection, when care is all about looking after the other person.

There are no rules for such moments; no guidelines on when and with whom and for how long and in what way you have to give someone that bit of attention or make them feel special. It mostly takes a well-trained eye to see what is needed and a sound heart that is capable of being moved by what the eye sees. And that's what it comes back to: virtue, the necessary complement to professional skills.

Mangomoments show us how important it is for social workers to be able to act as skilled companions. It's not just a question of 'what' happens – that it is performed professionally and with expertise – but also 'how' it is done. In other words, how someone in that care situation is cared for, reassured and guided. It seems so normal, but it really is vital.

So it's important to keep both the small and the big questions in view. Ethics in healthcare is not only about well-founded theories and pressing dilemmas, but also about how we should live with and for others on a daily basis. About how we can practice these virtuous attitudes in our day-to-day activities. And how organisations should go about creating a culture in which these attitudes are formed, maintained and strengthened.

Or as the renowned American ethicist Arthur Caplan puts it: "The ethics of the ordinary is just as much part of healthcare ethics as the ethics of the extraordinary." That's what we need to keep in mind, just like what the Judeo-French philosopher Emmanuel Levinas calls *la petite bonté* – little acts of kindness that take place between one person and another in very specific circumstances, in a very specific good deed that addresses a particular need of a specific Other. It's about respect and how people are treated, about the ability to pay attention to the Other. It's very specific, very partial, very real.

Grandmothers turning sadness into joy

Maria de los Ángeles Ghersi de Delgado
is grandmother and founder of the Abueladas movement in Venezuela. Abueladas is a naughty group of grandmothers living in a country where mangos are freely available.

Mangomoments are contextual and interactive – time, place, individual preferences, historical nuances, sociopolitical surroundings are just a few of our influencers that help to shape the choices we make as givers and influence our perception as receivers of these small, unexpected acts or gestures which are of great value in the care experience. It's a concept that can be translated and adapted way beyond care.

My context is Venezuela, a gorgeous South American nation where I was born and have since lived, where I saw my four children be born. Just to illustrate – located quite close to the equator, the weather varies minimally and there are no marked seasons. The average annual temperature in my city (Caracas) is a pleasant 24 degree Celsius – the Caribbean Sea is only thirty minutes away; the west of the country marks the start of the beautiful Andes mountain range, and the lush Amazon jungle in the south is the breathing lung of our continent. Furthermore, the country is home to the largest oil reserves on the planet. Despite its paradisiac description, Venezuela is imploding economically and socially – hyperinflation, criminality and lack of basic medicines, goods and services are just a few of the factors that have led to the country's largest ever emigration. In 2019, it was estimated that there were four million migrants and refugees from Venezuela. A sad story that has fragmented families regardless of their socioeconomic position. My context is one that challenges even the most psychologically resilient families to endure the unnatural breaks in family structure taking place – my children have all emigrated at different times to different countries, and my dreams of being a hands-on grandmother have been reduced to the few days or weeks I can see them every one or two years, and to the countless attempts to keep their attention for even five minutes on a monitor when we use technology to connect.

Every crisis presents opportunities, and my decision was to turn sadness into joy, a sense of loss and isolation into a sense of community and belonging, the risk of illness into the promotion of health and wellbeing. Abueladas was born in 2018, a movement of grandmothers with a clear vision – to improve the quality of life and the wellbeing of Venezuelan grandmothers across the globe, from a position of joy and towards transcendence. Abueladas is hard to translate, its meaning conveys kind of a naughty group of grandmothers conspiring for goodness. Through dialogue with daring grandmothers, we developed four primary drivers for our work – sharing and celebrating memories (through writing, videos and other means leveraging the best that online platforms and social media have to offer); sharing of strategies to connect affectively and effectively with our grandchildren who live abroad; sharing and disseminating traditions, such as our unique family recipes and others; and the development of supportive experiences and the development of community. This is where I see the clear translation into daily life – what Abueladas does is to create Mangomoments for grandmothers that promote health and wellbeing. From the pleasure of writing life's memories or family recipes as legacy for the next generation, to identifying how to surprise our grandkids virtually on special occasions, through to the incredibly fun weekly card games of quarterly laughing – drawing – pilates – yoga – meditation retreats that we host and promote, Abueladas is designed to be an ever renewable source of energy, a set of individual and communal Mangomoments that helps us transcend, find meaning, and navigate our national and local context of hopelessness.

You may wonder how in our imperfect translation and adaptation of Mangomoments to everyday life these moments, which sound as if always perfectly planned, are 'unexpected acts or gestures'. What is clearly unexpected is the magic that unfolds when we get together, when our dialogue and interactions take us to unexpected and unique mind and body places that help us develop resilience. It's the humanity of eye contact, of a warm embrace, of a kind word. It's the pursuit of a worthwhile life, the shared belief that despite what destiny has thrown at us, we still own our destiny. In a country where mangos are ubiquitous and freely available, as well as extraordinarily delicious, we will continue to build Mangomoments with the conviction that through these small acts and gestures that shape experience, we can somehow infect others with the sentiment of building a better society, a better country, a better future.

Does the dough still rise?

Jan Peers is emeritus professor of healthcare management at KU Leuven and was general manager at University Hospitals Leuven for many years. He was advisor to several Belgian ministers of social affairs and public health.

Mangomoments can most definitely occur in healthcare settings, but they do require a conducive context. Health, too, is the result of a complex system comprising many factors, which means it is not easy to change. For centuries, the options for caring for sick and vulnerable fellow human beings were very limited due to a lack of medical knowledge, with healthcare being mainly focused on 'caritas'. From the second half of the last century, new methods and techniques were introduced that brought healthcare into a more technical world. This resulted in a high degree of specialisation, which increased the importance of scientific, technical and innovative skills in employees. Today, increasing attention is once again being paid to the combination of scientific and technical skills, on the one hand, and the care aspect, on the other.

Given the importance of both social and economic factors on health, policy choices relating to wellbeing and prosperity need to take into account the efforts necessary for healthcare. Whoever makes the decisions within an organisation, policy is crucial, particularly right at the top. Within the healthcare sector, it is important to ensure that the best results are achieved through good organisation, and that all aspects of healthcare retain their value. This means that these choices need to ensure that all employees are given the opportunity to carry out their job as professionally as possible. Furthermore, the available knowledge and skills must be put to the best possible use to promote the health of the wider population through cooperation between healthcare professionals and organisations.

We must ensure that we continue to pay attention to both the hard and soft sides of care. Extra consideration for Mangomoments must not translate into excessive focus on the soft side, leaving less attention or energy for excellent technology or innovation. These two aspects must be kept in a healthy balance. In other words, it is through making a useful contribution in whatever way best suits their particular role that people find satisfaction in their professional lives.

Good patient care is achieved by combining many components. This requires coordination and cooperation between many professional groups to ensure that each patient's care is optimised. To bake a good loaf, you need to put the right ingredients together and then process them in the right way. In addition, the environment must be right and the dough must be given time to rest. It's the same for organisational development. You will never make a delicious pastry by simply putting flour next to milk, butter or yeast. It has to be processed in a favourable environment. Taking high-quality ingredients and doing nothing with them results in only one thing: the devaluation of the ingredients themselves.

An organisation, whether in the healthcare sector or elsewhere, will only continue to deliver good quality if it can retain its enthusiastic employees. Perhaps the greatest effect of the Mangomoment is that it gives employees the energy to keep on kneading the dough and shaping it into whatever the customer has ordered. If you stop getting those tiny, positive Mangomoments, the dough won't rise, or – worse still – after a while something will happen that will make the dough collapse. You can see that in the care sector as well. When someone makes a mistake or a patient safety incident accidentally occurs, that's exactly the time when the organisation and company need to keep supporting the people and keep the team together. If managers are able to do this in difficult times it results in staff with the psychological safety to do just that little bit more for the patient. Staff need the courage to colour outside the lines, in a positive sense, when it benefits the patient. So it's a question of daring to as well as wanting to and that calls for mutual trust in good times, but especially in bad.

Will and courage are necessary not only for the individual healthcare professional or for the further development and growth of healthcare as a whole, but also for every organisation, every society and every family. Mangomoments can help to create the context that allows us to face this complex challenge.

Mangomoments create energy for change

Jessica Perlo is director at the Institute for Healthcare Improvement in Boston and leads the Joy In Work movement.

Mangomoments at their core are about human connections and relationships. Where is this more important than in healthcare? I love the opportunity Mangomoments give us to improve healthcare not just for patients but also for one another. For many years, the Institute for Healthcare Improvement (IHI) has been promoting the transformative provocation to ask patients 'What matters to you?' in addition to 'What's the matter?' We also ask healthcare leaders to ask the healthcare workforce the same question when we focus on Joy in Work. Only by understanding what truly matters to staff and offering moments for connection will we be able to identify and remove barriers to joy, wellbeing, and connection.

Even after years of working on Joy at IHI, I am still sometimes daunted by the challenges our workforce is up against. These are the things that can feel insurmountable in the system like time and volume pressures, lack of control over work, poor processes and waste, miscommunication and a lack of trust – just to name a few. When I hear these things, my gut goes into 'fix it' mode and I can feel overwhelmed. Mangomoments reminds me to look for the values and interests of the people I work with, not just what's getting in the way. In doing so, we can think together about the smaller more incremental changes that can be made to improve our Joy in Work – our mangos. This is true whether we're talking to our staff or our patients. The question after we reflect on what really matters then becomes 'Okay, what can we do by next Tuesday to get us closer to that? Let's think together about changes'. This is not meant to ignore the larger issues that need to be addressed to mitigate burnout but looks to establish a foundation of meaning, purpose, camaraderie and equity. This is why 'Ask what matters' is the first step of the IHI Framework for Joy in Work and why Mangomoments are so important. It gives us an excuse to slow down, not make assumptions and reconnect to the people we work beside every day. Relationships, kindness, connection: these things are always available when we make the time.

What's more is it really works. One example from our work at IHI comes from the University of Virginia School of Nursing team who found that using this approach from the IHI Framework for Improving Joy in Work was more effective than the standard committee-driven process they were used to. In previous staff satisfaction surveys, employees identified a strong desire for time off, unencumbered by the expectation of responding to e-mail but little had been done about this. So, instead of another satisfaction survey they asked staff directly what they could test to respect each other's time out of the office. They discovered and tested a small change with a small group to see if it were possible to avoid sending e-mail to staff who were out of office and delaying routine e-mails from the weekend to the following week. The benefits were immediately evident, especially with their part-time and hourly staff who had been overloaded with e-mails during most of their time off. Soon the invitation was extended to all school employees with great success – even the dean adopted the practice. In a post-intervention survey, 80% of respondents reported improvement in respect for personal time off. Building on this success, the team is using this Framework and a relationship focused approach to address other longstanding problems to improve staff wellbeing and Joy in Work.

By working to create Mangomoments, and beginning our work together with asking 'What matters?', leaders at all levels engage in a form of appreciative inquiry that taps into strengths or bright spots, or what's already working in the organisation, that offers energy for change.

Mangos in the workplace

Luc Sels is Rector of KU Leuven, and a full professor at the Department of Work and Organisation Studies of the Faculty of Economics and Business. He is actively involved in policy consultation in the broad domain of labour market policy and is a member of the Belgian High Council for Employment. He is director of the Centre of Expertise for Labour Market Monitoring, which advises the Flemish government on labour market policy.

When I think and write about job satisfaction, I often draw on writings on the subject of what motivates people, and essays about how leadership inspires.

I'll start with motivation. In his book *The Surprising Truth about What Motivates Us*, Daniel Pink puts it into clear focus, highlighting purpose, mastery and autonomy as the forces that drive us. Employees need purpose or meaning. They want a mission, or at least the feeling that what they do is contributing to a higher goal such as better care, a great product, a sustainable world or a happy face. Mastery, the pleasure of doing something well and getting better at it, is important too. This doesn't necessarily have to be at the level of virtuosity – expertise is often sufficient. Finally, autonomy is all about being able to make decisions for yourself, in particular deciding how you are going to go about things. What it boils down to is being given, and taking up, a degree of freedom. Always having to do things because your leader says so eats away at meaning and mastery.

This brings us to leadership, a subject on which much has already been written. As a leader, how do you find your way through the proliferation of adjectives that precede this highly charged word? Adjectives like autocratic, vulnerable, charismatic, visionary, task-oriented, relational, situational, contextual, inclusive, serving, spiritual, transformational, authentic and whatever else you care to add to the list. Personally, I prefer to stay out of it. For me, it's more useful to focus on the tools and strategies that leaders have available to them to help them shape and flesh out the experience of mastery, meaning and autonomy, such as:

Encouraging employees to express their ideas, and genuinely considering their suggestions, even if you don't entirely agree with them. Adopting a consultative attitude that encourages employees to engage with the issues that you as a 'leader' are dealing with or the problems you are up against. Creating an environment in which mistakes are discussed rather than jumped upon and punished. Sincerely believing that all, or almost all, employees have the ability to improve. Daring to set high expectations. Nurturing passion by conferring challenging responsibilities. Daring to tell the hard truth and being strict, but at the same time admitting your own mistakes and thus creating a psychologically safe environment in which employees are encouraged to do the same. Opting for shared leadership. Not hesitating to recognise when others have more expertise than you have. Staying true to yourself. Avoiding responding defensively to criticism. Communicating transparently.

As you can see, it's not so difficult to get the building blocks of human motivation and the outlines of real leadership down on paper. But I still ask myself whether this really captures all the elements of pure Joy in Work. I personally doubt it. So, what's missing? Well, I wonder whether, in the world of work, we are giving enough attention to the everyday, to consideration, to the unexpected and the surprise, to the little courtesy and the warm gesture. To Mangomoments. To asking about the photo next to your colleague's computer screen and being genuinely interested in the answer. To the little compliment without any specific outcome in mind. To the treat, for no reason. To the 'just because'. To giving your boss a pat on the back (believe me, they need it too). To stepping in and helping out, spontaneously and without any expectation of the favour being returned. To the listening ear, even though the clock is ticking and targets are lurking around the corner. To prioritising connectedness, just for once.

We have a hard time with Mangomoments at work. Colleagues are not the same as patients. The human suffering of a patient naturally invokes more in the way of warm gestures and reassuring words. After all, even a hardened and seasoned surgeon cannot help but be moved by the fear in someone's eyes or dread of loss they are clearly feeling. In the world of work, we are not dependent on care in the same way. Moreover, relationships in a care setting are often more short-lived than those in the workplace, which often endure over long periods. This can be a wonderful thing but it has the downside that, over time, habits can set in and routines and patterns become entrenched. It's easy to forget to pay attention to the unusual, the surprise or the unique moment.

Moreover, in the world of work, Mangomoments are sometimes at odds with the desire for fairness. If someone is paid a lot of attention, this can easily be perceived as others being neglected. If one person gets a mango and others don't it can look like preferential treatment, favouritism, unequal opportunities or imbalance in working relationships. And the world of work is often one of *deals* and *tit for tat*, with attention to the employee being seen as an investment that needs to have a payback. Little is done for nothing; often there is an expectation of more engagement, more effort, more involvement, more commitment. We want something in return.

Even when we try to meet the individual needs of the employee in the most personal way possible, we are often still thinking in terms of a *deal*. This can be the case for the engineer who gets to take her underwater photography course on educational leave, despite this not being the normal practice, or for the young father who is allowed to work different hours because it suits him better. Or when we go along with the wishes of that one employee who always gives their all, but is dead set on being on their surfboard as soon as the wind is right. It's a wonderful thing that more space is being found in the workplace for this kind of personal treatment, but often it is part of a deal and only comes about because we're expecting it to deliver some kind of added value. Give and take.

By contrast, true Mangomoments – surprising, disarming and simply heart-warming gestures without any ulterior motive – are still all too rare in the workplace. This is why I hope this book will be read outside the world of care and welfare by those in positions of responsibility within our companies and organisations who are working to achieve a *great place to work*.

CLOSING WORDS

MANGO moment

Towards a society rich in Mangomoments and free of cancer

Jean-Jacques Cassiman is emeritus professor of medical genetics at KU Leuven and chairman of Kom op tegen Kanker (Stand up to Cancer).

Marc Michils is managing director of Stand up to Cancer.

Kom op tegen Kanker

At the age of 93, Stéphane Hessel, former ambassador of the United Nations and champion of human rights, wrote the excellent pamphlet *Indignez-vous*, inciting us to be and remain outraged. It's a wonderful thing that a man who had experienced so much was still able to feel indignation about injustices and failings. We must never accept the status quo. Open and critical thinking are the keys to progress. Shortly after *Indignez-vous*, *Engagez-vous* was published, and it's clear that these two concepts are perfect counterparts. Outrage and engagement are also what drive everyone involved in Stand up to Cancer. We are striving to build a cancer-free world through research, information and preventative measures, psychosocial initiatives and policy work and will keep on doing so until we are no longer losing our loved ones to cancer. Until we can guarantee 100% quality of life for every patient during and after cancer.

The Mangomoment project of Kris Vanhaecht and his team must have grown out of the same sense of outrage. Viviane, the lady who was interviewed so beautifully by Annemie Struyf, was certainly surrounded by the best medical care. But her face still lit up when Annemie Struyf came in with a mango in answer to her question 'So, Viviane, what can I do for you?' Good care is not just about avoiding adverse events or providing optimal physical care, it is also about trying to achieve the very best support and psychosocial care. Kris Vanhaecht realised that there was still scope for a whole waiting room full of improvements in this area. Every medical specialist aims to do their utmost for their patients, to take care of them in all senses of the word, as human beings as well as patients. How can we do even more to make our patients happy? How can we ensure that they all experience many Vivian moments? Thus, the Mangomoment project was born. As is often the case with innovations, this was a coincidental but massively significant side-effect of another story: Annemie Struyf's beautiful interview with Viviane. It was like when Alexander Fleming accidentally discovered penicillin in 1928. The rest is history: Kris Vanhaecht and his team initiated a pilot project, Stand up to Cancer linked a campaign to it, the project was scaled up to reach a broader audience, and now there is a book. Hopefully this will be the trigger for many examples of good practice, education and training for all professionals in the healthcare system as a whole, which will give rise to even better and more efficient healthcare. For all patients facing cancer or any other disease. With us and elsewhere.

The essence of a Mangomoment lies not in enjoying a mango, for example, but in looking for those small moments of beauty that awaken feelings of optimism in cancer patients. It's not about grand gestures, it's about that spark of connection that creates a small, meaningful, virtuous moment between the patient and their (healthcare) environment. It's also about the positive effect that you can see in the faces of patients who take part in Stand up to Cancer's 1,000 km cycle ride or spot amongst those who come to recount their story into the microphones of Warmste Week, an initiative of the Flemisch public Broadcast Organisation VRT. Everybody taking care of everybody else. In its ambition to create a cancer-free society, Stand up to Cancer thus invests not only in preventing and fighting cancer, but also in making illness more bearable. This can take the form of improved support and care for the human being behind the patient based on psychosocial projects such as this Mangomoment project. But it can also be about financing care organisations, peer groups, care volunteers, youth weeks, a weekend in Brussels and children's camps.

We can all learn a lot from cancer patients, from their willpower, positive thinking and vulnerability. The misery that cancer patients have to go through is a source of inspiration for greater understanding, appreciation and humanity. Particularly in these times of change and uncertainty, we are crying out for more moments of solidarity and optimism. More Mangomoments for patients and for society as a whole. The enormous potential for solidarity that exists is demonstrated by the increasing engagement in initiatives such as Stand up to Cancer, Warmste week and all the others. And this is in spite of – or perhaps thanks to – the increasing individualisation and polarisation of society. Could it be a silent protest against the conflict model our society increasingly seems to at risk of evolving towards? It's a great pleasure to give and to help, and these actions bestow a wonderful feeling of happiness on both 'giver' and 'receiver'. So let this be a plea for the reappraisal of connection and empathy so that we can move towards a society that is free of cancer and rich in Mangomoments.